Schönbrunn Palace
The State Apartments

Georg Kugler

Schönbrunn Palace
The State Apartments

Published by
Schloß Schönbrunn Kultur- und Betriebsges.m.b.H.

Verlag Christian Brandstätter

1st edition in November 1995

Layout and jacket design by Bohatsch and Schedler,
produced, typeset and photographic reproductions by pd/MCA.
Editor: Barbara Sternthal
Technical editor: Franz Hanns
Translated by Sophie Francis Kidd
Production: Druckerei Gutenberg in Wiener Neustadt.
Set in Utopia

ISBN 3-85447-628-0

Schloß Schönbrunn
Kultur- und Betriebsges.m.b.H.
A-1130 Wien, Schloß Schönbrunn

Contents

History of the Palace

History of the Palace

Schönbrunn – a Baroque summer palace

The famous Equestrian Ballet in the inner courtyard of the Vienna Hofburg is an example of a Baroque Gesamtkunstwerk: *architecture, painting, music and dance combine to form a magnificent spectacle.*

Of the world of the European Baroque, it is principally the works belonging to the fine arts that have become the natural intellectual and cultural property of Europe, both in the Protestant north and west as well as the Catholic centre and south of the continent. The literature of the 17th and early 18th centuries on the other hand (with the exception of French literature), has been almost wholly forgotten; German literary Baroque lives on only in Church liturgy and a few folk songs. The music of this age was also rarely heard until the advent of the long-playing record led to its rediscovery on a wide scale. By contrast, the fine arts live on in the great architecture of the age which towered above and subsumed sculpture, painting and all the manual arts and crafts.

It is the domed churches and the proud palaces in the cities, the splendid monasteries and the magnificent castles in the country, set in landscaped surroundings which are visited and admired by countless people, both as works of art and as monuments to the high culture of a bygone age. Princely summer palaces always exercise a special attraction since their most important characteristic, the combination of architecture and landscape, that is, of art and nature, is a feature which speaks to and interests the people of our time as well.

The term »Baroque« comes from history of art, but as this style encompasses all areas of European secular and ecclesiastical culture in the 17th century, we speak of a Baroque style of life. In political terms it was an age of princely absolutism and centrally-controlled states, when these states undertook massive efforts to achieve supremacy in Europe by fighting wars lasting for decades. In art, too, there was a noticeable tendency towards inclusiveness, even a fusion of all the different forms of visual art: architecture, sculpture and painting did not merely coexist beside one other, but combined to form a common creation, with one form even representing or replacing another. Façades of buildings break out in sculptural details which are in turn continued or imitated by painting that fills the domes and ceilings with the illusion of infinite architecture. It is no longer the quiet harmony of the Renaissance that was being aimed for, but a powerful fusion of all forces. It leads to a heightened sense of life, which is in its turn experienced as harmonious.

Versailles, the most important of all the palaces built in this age, became the model for countless other palaces in Europe. In Germany, where so many princely residences had been destroyed in the course of the Thirty Years' War, an intense period of building activity began. The French models were particularly influential in the Protestant north of Germany. In Vienna, capital city and imperial seat, the situation was completely different: not only were Italian architects already well-established in the city, but after the siege of Vienna by the Turks in 1683, when a wealth of opportunities arose for architects, they were joined by Austrian artists, who absorbed impulses from Italian and French art, thereby creating the specifically Austrian Baroque style which we also encounter at Schönbrunn Palace.

Emperor Leopold I and Empress Margareta Teresa as Acis and Galatea in a performance of La Galatea *on the occasion of their marriage in 1667. Painting by Jan Thomas.*

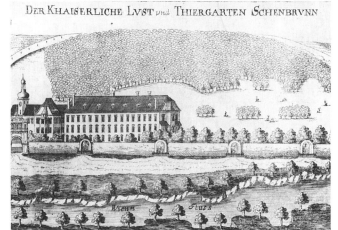

The Katterburg, the former imperial hunting lodge on the banks of the River Wien. It was the forerunner of the present palace at Schönbrunn. Engraving by Georg Matthäus Vischer, 1672.

Since the 16th century the Habsburg rulers had owned a hunting lodge, called the Katterburg, situated in extensive grounds on the banks of the River Wien to the west of Vienna, near the village of Hietzing. At the beginning of the 17th century, Emperor Matthias discovered a spring there, the waters of which were so highly estimated that a well was built round it and decorated with the statue of a nymph, and the name Schönbrunn (The Beautiful Spring) was given to the place. The hunting lodge, fountain, park and hunting grounds were destroyed in the Turkish siege of 1683. The name, however, was retained for the great new palace that was gradually built on this site over several decades. The stone with the monogramme of Emperor Matthias is still to be found by the spring in the grotto later built to enclose it.

Stone slab bearing the monogramme of Emperor Matthias, who discovered the spring at Schönbrunn.

The future emperor Joseph I as a youthfully impetuous rider in the pose of victor over the Turks. This small, ivory equestrian figure was executed by Matthias Steinle in 1693. It is one of the finest works of sculpture produced in the Austrian Baroque.

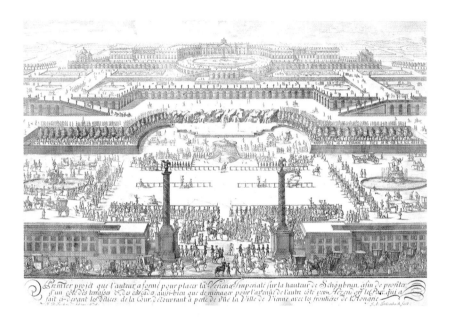

Premier projet que l'auteur a formé pour placer la Venerie Imperiale sur la hauteur de Schönbrun, afin de profiter d'un côté des terrasses & des cascades, aussi-bien que de menager pour l'avenüe de l'autre côte vers Hetzen, qui la dua, qui a fait a-devant les délices de la Cour, découvrant a perte de vüe la Ville de Vienne avec les frontières de la Hongrie.

Johann Bernhard
Fischer von Erlach:
Initial design for
the imperial
summer residence
at Schönbrunn,
1688.

The commission to design a new palace to replace the Katter-burg was entrusted to Johann Bernhard Fischer von Erlach (1656-1723). He had spent 16 years in Rome where he had been the pupil of Gianlorenzo Bernini, the famous architect and sculptor. In the 1680s he was appointed tutor to Crown Prince Joseph. Despite his youth, Fischer von Erlach was already regarded as one of the greatest architects of the age and since he was not merely a master builder but also possessed a profound knowledge of historical architecture, he seemed ideally suited to teach the principles of his art to the young prince. In 1688 he designed a huge palace for his pupil, larger than Versailles, a design which can only be described as verging on the fantastic. It corresponded to the lofty plans of the Crown Prince and the bold ambition of its author, but bore little relation to practical possibilities. The designs for this building, sited on a natural eminence, were underpinned by the idea of an imperial residence reflecting the feeling of German national identity which had suddenly flared up again at the end of the 17th century. It had been ignited by two events: on the one hand by the occupation of the free imperial city of Strasbourg by Louis XIV's troops in peacetime (1681) and on the other by the siege of the imperial capital of Vienna by the Turkish army in 1683. Following the relief of Vienna, a victorious campaign against the French and the Turks began, and confidence and a sense of security gradually returned. The readiness to experiment with new architectural styles received

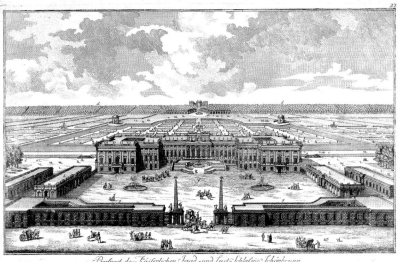

Prospect der Käiserlichen Jagd-und Lust-Schlosses Schönbrunn

a. der große Saal. b. Capelle. c. Eingang zum Lustgarten d. Thiergarten. e. Fasanen Wald. f. Tournier-Platz. g. Wohnung der Bedienten. h. Stelle für die Pferd. i. der Bediennt Pferd. k. Wagenremise.

Johann Bernhard Fischer von Erlach: Second design for the imperial summer residence at Schönbrunn, 1696.

added impetus from the fact that building sites of all sizes had arisen in and around Vienna through the destruction that had taken place during the siege. Soon the nobility was vying with the Emperor to build larger, more magnificent and multifarious edifices.

The political and artistic developments after 1683 had a lasting influence on the young Archduke Joseph; he became the focus of corresponding expectations which he was, however, unable to fulfil in his short reign (1705-1711). At all events, the gigantic palace on the hill above the River Wien, the site where the Gloriette was to be built years later, was nothing more than an extravagant product of the imagination, the building of which even Joseph, lover of magnificence though he was, was unwilling to sanction. A few years after his first design, Fischer von Erlach submitted a second set of much simpler and thus realistic plans. The »hunting lodge« was moved down into the valley, while the rise was to be crowned with a pavilion only. In 1696, building was begun on Schönbrunn according to these plans.

Many princely summer palaces of the Baroque share certain characteristic elements and forms which we also encounter in Schönbrunn. Thus the whole complex is symmetrical and extends over several buildings which are grouped around a main building. The latter has two different façades: one on the side of the courtyard, facing the city, and the other facing the gardens. On the courtyard side, the central section dominates by virtue of its greater height and the sculptural elements with which it is decorated. These are repeated on the ends of the wings of this section, albeit in a more restrained style. Here further side wings join the main section at right angles - in Schönbrunn these are free-standing buildings - which enclose a large courtyard known as the »Ehrenhof«, literally »Court of Honour« or Parade Court. This served to accommodate the arrival of the great six-horse carriages, and was where carousels were set up and open-air celebrations held. On the garden side the façade is less differentiated. Following a straight line, it forms the limit of the parterre, from which all the carriageways and paths lead into the gardens, the entire complex of which can be seen from this point.

The first part of the palace to be built was the central section, and a garden was laid out by Jean Trehet, most probably designed to harmonise with Fischer von Erlach's plans. The landscape gardener had studied a number of French parks and had also brought 1,000 saplings and the model of an irrigation system for Schönbrunn from Paris. As early as 1700 the palace and gardens were being shown to foreign visitors, and festivities, receptions and even a tournament were held in the Parade Court. Schönbrunn was regarded as a hunting lodge which was only used for a few days or even sometimes only a period of hours. The dense forests which extended around Hietzing determined the use to which Schönbrunn was put. Hunting was regarded as the noblest sport of princes, and horses played an important role, as indeed they did in day-to-day life as well. The noble steed was the prince's companion and was held in high esteem, bred for performance and immortalised in oils! The Equestrian Room of the palace still bears witness to this imperial passion with its large series of portraits of horses bearing the names and dates of the animals. Artists who specialised in painting horses and dogs, such as the Dutch Hamilton brothers, devoted their lives exclusively to this task in their capacity as »Court Animal Painters«. Fischer von Erlach's designs included stabling for 400 horses and numerous carriages. Although work on the palace was delayed by lack of funds due to the wars against France, building continued on Schönbrunn throughout Joseph I's reign. However, after his death in 1711, building was stopped and his widow Wilhelmine Amalie inherited the palace, which remained the court's residence in summer as well as serving to accommodate royal visitors and hunting parties. In 1728 the Emperor's widow gave it to her brother-in-law, Emperor Charles VI, and retired to a convent. The new ruler had no especial interest in Schönbrunn and used it only occasionally as a hunting lodge. A painting by Johann Georg Hamilton of partridges in the park at Schön-

View of Schönbrunn Palace, depicted in the background of a painting by Johann Georg Hamilton, 1732.

The Palace Designed by Fischer von Erlach

brunn reveals the appearance of the palace around 1732. The flat roof of the elegant summer palace had to be replaced soon afterwards with a pitched roof more appropriate to the northern climate. Whatever else was altered at that time is not known, for the palace only awoke from its »hundred-year sleep« when a new generation entered the political stage.

In 1736 Archduchess Maria Theresa (b. 1717), the eldest daughter of Emperor Charles VI, married Duke Francis Stephen of Lorraine, whom she had known since her childhood. Her succession to the vast Habsburg lands had been secured by a special law known as the Pragmatic Sanction, and as a result of agreements negotiated with other states by the Emperor, the female succession had been recognised on an international level as well. She was the richest heiress in Europe and her husband could count on a good chance of becoming Roman-German King and Emperor. The young couple, who thought all the cares and troubles of state affairs in the distant future, were permitted to establish their residence at Schönbrunn, the long-neglected hunting lodge. Maria Theresa must have grown to love it, for when her father died in 1740 and she became regent of the Austrian Hereditary Lands at an unexpectedly early date, she planned not only to have it finished immediately but also to have it completely remodelled.

However, first of all economies proved to be necessary, for, just as the elderly Prince Eugene had foreseen, the young heiress' succession was not to go unchallenged, despite all the treaties. By the time Maria Theresa was crowned Queen of Hungary in Pressburg, she was already at war with Frederick II of Prussia. She survived this baptism of fire and secured the existence of her state, but the rich province of Silesia was lost.

In the meantime, the office of Roman-German Emperor had been given not to her husband Francis Stephen, but to the Bavarian Elector Karl Albrecht, who died shortly afterwards in 1745, however. Francis Stephen, by this time Grand Duke of Tuscany, was then duly elected and the Viennese court became once more a seat of empire. The dignity of the imperial family and the state demanded the appropriate external trappings of magnificence. In 1743, while the Austrians were successfully advancing against the Bavarian and French forces, Nikolaus Pacassi, a young architect from Wiener Neustadt, was drawing up plans to alter Schönbrunn Palace completely, both inside and out.

Maria Theresa as an eleven-year-old archduchess, the most brilliant match in Europe. Painting by Andreas Möller, c. 1727.

The rebuilding of Schönbrunn had several aims: the palace was to be enlarged and the interior completely altered to accommodate the changed needs of permanent residence and the exterior was to be adapted to contemporary taste. The most radical exterior alteration was the addition of an upper storey above the main floor of the wings, together with the removal of the pitched roof to something approximating the original roof form intended by Fischer von Erlach. For the interior, Pacassi had the original idea of replacing the existing and conventional large ceremonial hall at the centre of the palace with two rooms of different sizes which could be used together or separately: the two famous galleries. The Great Gallery lies on the courtyard side and is reached by the large exterior staircase or perron also built at that time, under which an open driveway with five arches extends to the other side of the palace. Whereas in Baroque times carriages drove up to the palace over ramps, the ceremonial protocol of the Rococo demanded that they drove up to an open stairway or into a hall leading to staircases. Pacassi therefore replaced a dining room with a large stair hall. The original ceiling, painted by the Venetian artist Sebastiano Ricci in 1700, was preserved and the fresco can still be seen by visitors today when they ascend the Blue Staircase to the imperial apartments.

The Small Gallery lies on the garden side of the palace, parallel to the Great Gallery and joined to the latter by three arches. Both galleries are surrounded by both grand as well as more intimate rooms: the Hall of Ceremonies, the Carousel Room and the Lantern Room on the one hand and the two Chinese Cabinets and the Equestrian Room on the other.

Since Maria Theresa intended to spend most of the year at Schönbrunn, it was she who largely determined the interior arrangement of the palace and the use to which the various rooms were to be put. The Prussian envoy Count Podewils later reported to his king that »*She takes pleasure in building without having any understanding of it, to which the house that she has had built at Schönbrunn bears witness.*« This malicious comment refers to the fact that Schönbrunn was not altered according to the traditional architectonic principles for buildings of this type, but that Maria Theresa had had a family residence built. A palace that was to be lived in for the major part of the year needed many more rooms than usual to accommodate the court and its servants, which together numbered almost 1,000 persons. The Empress' growing family needed ever larger living quarters. The children of the imperial couple - ten out of sixteen lived to adulthood - grew up almost exclusively at Schönbrunn. It was not until 1768 that Maria Karolina left the court to follow her husband to Naples. Maria Christine, who had married in 1760, spent the major part of her life in Vienna with her husband, two daughters never married and remained at the Viennese court, as did the eldest son and later co-regent, Joseph II. Each member of the imperial family had five rooms at their disposal, married couples had ten. According to the rules of court ceremonial these consisted of a waiting room and audience room (also called the first and second *anticamera*), a salon and a combined drawing-room and bedroom. These apartments were mostly on the ground floor. In addition to this, visitors' quarters were needed, as well as handsomely-appointed rooms that were suitable for the numerous family celebrations as well as for audiences and conferences. The birthdays and name-days of family members, the apostles' and saints' days, the great church festivals and commemoration days of important events were not merely marked by attendance at Holy Mass in one of the churches in Vienna or outside the city; they were also celebrated within the family circle in the Hofburg or at Schönbrunn.

Depending on the time of year and the weather, according to the numbers or importance of the visitors but above all according to the type of celebration, the state rooms could be adapted as required in a short space of time. Now as then, these rooms were normally empty and furniture was brought in as needed: a table for twelve in a small room, a banqueting table for sixty in the Hall of Ceremonies or the Small Gallery, and when several hundred guests were invited, smaller tables were set up in all the large rooms. If there was to be a serenata, ballet or dramatic performance after a reception, with a few practised moves a scene change as it were could be swiftly effected, seating set up, curtains raised and so on. If dancing was on the programme, card tables had to be set up for those who were disinclined to participate, and above all, there had to be sufficient facilities for the long periods of just waiting around which court life involved. This might be in the case of

The Singspiel Il parnasso confuso *by Christoph Willibald von Gluck. A performance given in the Hall of Ceremonies by Maria Theresa's children on the occasion of the marriage of Emperor Joseph II to Archduchess Maria Josepha of Bavaria, 1765.*

the great religious festivals, when the ceremonies were taking place three rooms ahead and those attending were only admitted to pay their respects after hours of waiting, or when audiences were given and there were many other people to be received, or in the expectation of the Empress being delivered of a child, when the noble well-wishers often had to haunt the antechambers for half the night.

At all the doors, on the landings of the staircases and in the corridors stood lackeys or guardsmen, and before the palace, in the Parade Court and along all the roads of approach, stood the state coaches of the court officials, ministers and invited guests together with the carriages of those accompanying them. There were hundreds of lackeys and coachmen who waited at the ready, holding their horses' heads. They all waited, hour after hour.

In the 18th century there was an especial predilection for marking political events with a celebration at court. These celebrations always assumed the character of a family party at the court of Empress Maria Theresa, partly because this was in keeping with her nature and partly because she always included her children, even when they were still quite small. She also cultivated a personal relationship with her ladies-in-waiting and treated her chambermaids with almost maternal solicitude. The large painting which gives the so-called Carousel Room its name commemorates one of these celebrations, in which all of these attendants at court took part.

Scene from the ballet Il trionfo d'amore *by Florian Leopold Gassmann, performed by Maria Theresa's children, 1765.*

Schönbrunn after the second stage of alterations by Pacassi. Painting by Bernard Bellotto, called Canaletto, c. 1760.

Pacassi's alterations were completed in 1749. The new disposition and decoration of the rooms were master-strokes of ingenuity. However, the influence of the Empress on these alterations should not be underestimated. The characteristic decorative feature of the rooms in the palace is the vigorous exuberance of the »rocaille« style, which is, however, more restrained and harmonious in comparison to German palaces of the same era. Already present in the Baroque art of Charles VI's era, this harmony also expresses the typical Habsburg characteristic of moderation and dignified simplicity in the personal sphere. The office and dignity of the imperial family naturally demanded pomp and circumstance for the court in its representative functions, but the individual was expected to observe the precepts of simplicity and moderation. This conduct was traditional on both sides of the dynasty, exemplified both by the »German« Maximilian I and the »Spaniards« Charles V and Philip II.

A summer residence like Schönbrunn was an ideal setting for both forms of expression of the Habsburg identity. In Maria Theresa's case there was in addition her natural sense of family. She wanted her children to be the focus of festivities of all kinds, of theatricals, concerts and ballet. To adapt Schönbrunn in this sense was her especial concern.

By contrast, the Emperor had no influence on the rebuilding of the palace, nor did he contribute to its financing. His interest lay entirely in the natural world together with its investigation and classification, and it is with the foundation of the Zoo and the Botanical or »Dutch« Garden that his name is linked. For the Empress, however, the furnishing and decora-

Coronation banquet in the Römer in Frankfurt, 1764. Emperor Francis Stephen and the newly-crowned Roman King, Joseph II, are seated at the high table. Painting by Martin van Meytens.

tion of the palace remained a central concern during her whole life, and a mere decade after the major alterations had been completed she had the two galleries altered again. They were given shallow vaulting which was decorated by the Italian painter Gregorio Guglielmi in the years 1760 to 1762 with frescoes depicting historico-allegorical subjects, in which the Imperial couple make a wholly natural appearance as actors in an historical event.

This concept of history led the Empress to commission her court painter Martin von Meytens from 1760 onwards to execute works which recorded important events in the history of state and family. Today we encounter a number of these impressive paintings where the Empress had them set into the walls at a later date, thereby destroying the interiors of these rooms which had originated from the time of her youth. This happened as a result of an event which was extremely painful for Maria Theresa, the death of Francis Stephen, her beloved husband, in 1765. For his widow, to whom the family was the basis of all political and artistic endeavours, his death necessarily brought drastic changes. She began to remodel the »*retirada*«, as the private apartments of her husband were known. It was then that the apartments in the east wing adjacent to the Hall of Ceremonies were given these sumptuous interiors at the hands of important architects, painters and craftsmen.

Schönbrunn – Monument to a Dynasty

During the latter years of her life, Maria Theresa was increasingly forced to listen to the opinion of her son, Emperor Joseph II, not only as far as affairs of state were concerned but also with regard to the building at Schönbrunn. He was her co-regent in the Austrian Lands and was no friend of extravagant building projects. His particular concern was to practise economy and ensure the distribution of financial resources to projects which served the common good of the state and his subjects.

Under his rule factories and mills, hospitals and schools, roads and canals were built, but no palaces. However, these projects were always a continuation of his mother's enterprises and Joseph was well aware of this.

Ceremonial entry of Emperor Francis Stephen and Archduke Joseph into Frankfurt, 1764. Painting by Martin van Meytens.

Thus on occasion he would merely assume a sceptical viewpoint towards his mother's plans for Schönbrunn, although he would have preferred different aspects and projects realised.

It was in these circumstances that Maria Theresa began planning a comprehensive redesigning of the gardens with architectural elements and sculptures according to the most modern principles. However, she was beset with uncertainty as to whether this would be successful or not. She expresses this in a letter to her daughter Marie Antoinette as follows: »*I quite understand that you cannot imagine the changes on the hill at Schönbrunn. They only exist on paper and will never be carried out! You know that the Emperor* (Joseph II) *does not love Schön-*

brunn, and at my age it would be ridiculous to begin such a work. As yet there is nothing at all on the hill, no building; I have merely had a large reservoir made so that opposite the house (i.e. palace), *at the end of the parterre, we may have a fountain. I hope that it will play in two years' time; I propose to decorate the parterre with statues.«*

Empress Maria Theresa dressed in mourning, holding a plan of Schönbrunn. Painting by Anton von Maron, 1773.

What had the park been like up to this point? What effect were the changes to have and whom were they intended to benefit? In order to realise the significance of the idea which underlay the redesigning of the palace gardens, it is necessary to explain the function of the gardens as well as their relationship to the palace and importance for courtly life.

It was the park at Versailles, the residential palace of King Louis XIV of France, laid out by the architect Le Nôtre in the second half of the 17th century, that provided the model for the garden as an integral part of the Baroque summer palace. It reflected the spirit of an age in which the natural sciences had made significant progress and at the same time acquired high prestige in society. The age was pervaded by the conviction that man could have mastery over Nature.

The Baroque garden is basically nothing other than applied science, Nature as ordered and shaped by the human mind. This type of park, like science itself, had its precursors in Italy. The self-assurance of Renaissance man had acquired a new relationship to nature; he knew more about it and admired its beauty like that of a work of art. The princely collections of the Renaissance consisted to a large degree of a diversity of objects and materials from nature, for example the shells of sea creatures, coral and coconut shells, ostrich eggs and rhinoceros horns. They were, however, mostly transformed into artefacts, for example as skilfully-wrought vessels or decorative centre-pieces. Man as artist and craftsman »embellished« the mira-culous gifts of Nature. The contemporary name by which these collections were known, *Kunst- und Wunderkammer* (Cabinets of Art and Curiosities), expresses this concept aptly. It also informed the designs of the Italian and French gardens. The interplay between gardens and large-scale architecture gives the latter a monumental aspect, not only in terms of scale but also in terms of their expressive programmme.

All parts of the park are connected with one another by avenues laid out symmetrically along the main axis of the palace, a design which is comprehensible not only in geometric but also optical terms. At the point of intersection of these axes lie basins with stone figures or fountains, and each one is terminated by a statue or building. The ground-plan of the park is formed by areas in which flowerbeds and lawns, ornamental shrubberies and tall trees alternate according to a carefully-considered design. The simple logic of the geometrical figures thus created was regarded as a precondition for truth and beauty.

The four elements are integrated into the design for the gardens. From the earth, represented by the leafy, artificially clipped walls of trees and the flowerbeds, arises the second element, living water, which enlivens the design of the garden. The gradient of the terrain was exploited to create cascades which flow into larger and smaller basins connected by channels. These were the setting for splendid nocturnal festivities, mock naval battles accompanied by music - an effect of the third element, air - and theatrical or ballet performances on floating islands. When darkness fell the fourth element brought all these festivities to a climax in the form of elaborate firework displays. These celebrations were not only enthusiastically enjoyed on the occasion itself but alsorecorded in contemporary descriptions and works of art.

The gardens laid out by Jean Trehet for Joseph I at Schönbrunn were planted with 1,000 saplings, and a machine was constructed to pump water up the slope for the cascades.

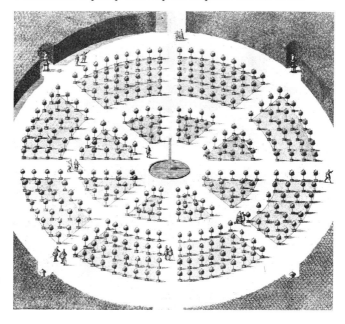

The new orangery, part of the original gardens at the beginning of the 18th century.

The Gardens at Schönbrunn
Palace and gardens as a conceptual unity

Essentially, however, Trehet only landscaped the parterre. Behind this lay the dark backdrop of the forest, the hunting grounds which stretched away to the south-west. The rebuilding of the palace by Pacassi also involved the enlargement of the gardens and the creation both of a large basin lying on the palace axis in the parterre as well as of a number of special features such as a maze (known as the labyrinth), a rose garden and the pheasantry which was the forerunner of the menagerie that was the special concern of Francis Stephen of Lorraine.

A painting from 1760 by the artist Bernardo Bellotto records the parterre as it looked at that time. The star-shaped basin in front of the palace is visible and in the bottom left-hand corner is the »labyrinth«. The lawns were laid out without floral decoration in an elaborate pattern resembling a carpet and along the central axis there were orange trees planted in wooden tubs, which had to be overwintered in the orangery. In the foreground of the painting there are gardeners at work, some of them rolling the gravel paths. How many people were

Details from the painting by Bernard Bellotto showing Schönbrunn in 1760 from the garden side.

needed to maintain these gardens! How many eked out an existence on the meagre pittance they received for their labour!

The late Baroque gardens as Bellotto recorded them were, little more than a decade later, to be altered and enlarged on the wishes of Maria Theresa. It was not merely to become something merely bigger, more beautiful and even more delightful, but was to satisfy entirely new demands according to the philosophical, aesthetic and pedagogical ideas of the second half of the 18th century.

Whereas the architectonically constructed landscape of the Baroque garden had been stage and foil for a courtly society which was sufficient to itself, from now on the palace at Schönbrunn, together with the gardens, zoo and Botanical Gardens, were to form a conceptual unity with national and political import. The park was therefore to be open to everybody. Maria Theresa stood between the two worlds of the self-confident Baroque on the one hand and the reflectiveness and enlightenment of the Rococo on the other. Under the influence of her husband Francis Stephen, she had devoted herself with interest to natural science collections and research expeditions. She promoted the foundation of what was later to become the Natural History Museum, while at the same time commissioning Johann Bergl's murals on the ground floor with their aesthetically and artistically sophisticated view of nature.

Her son Joseph II, on the other hand, was an enlightened monarch, albeit a despot who believed he knew what was best for the state and the happiness of his people.

His State Chancellor, Prince Wenzel Anton Kaunitz, shared his convictions despite belonging to an older generation. Although neither man was happy about Maria Theresa's plans for redesigning the gardens at Schönbrunn, they grasped the opportunity to steer the enterprise in the direction they favoured. The gardens were intended to represent a mythological and historical illustration of nature, and, as was so typical of that age, to be didactic in purpose. Beauty without aim and reason was not to be countenanced! Emperor Joseph II agreed to Maria Theresa entrusting this last great phase of building from 1765 to the architect Ferdinand von Hohenberg. The statuary work was executed by Wilhelm Beyer with the aid of several assistants from 1772 onwards, according to a plan drawn up by the Emperor and his State Chancellor in person.

Joseph II also turned his interest again to the zoo. His father, Francis Stephen, had had this laid out at the south-western edge of the park in 1751 after designs by the Lorrainese architect Jean Nicolas Jadot. Thirteen enclosures had been erected in a circle around an octagonal pavilion. The enclosures, which were separated from one another by walls, had runs equipped with pools and were enclosed by bars towards the pavilion. This historic zoo still exists today, although it has been extended by almost every succeeding generation. New

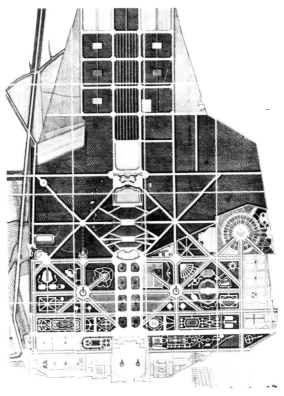

This design for the gardens was laid out by the court gardener Franz Boos after the remodelling of 1780 had been completed.

Emperor Francis Stephen and Empress Maria Theresa at work in the garden. Ink drawing by Franz Walter.

animals were constantly being added, either in the form of purchases, diplomatic gifts or as specimens brought back from expeditions. The Botanical Garden was also enlarged: in 1788 Joseph II had an arboretum planted as an extension of the Dutch Garden.

An example of the didactic features created at this time was an educational garden in which there were 400 plants arranged according to genus, species and subspecies after the botanical system of classification created by the Swedish naturalist Linnaeus. Later an Alpine garden was added to the Tyrolean Garden. Both served as practical instruction in botany and gardening for the children at court as well as providing a facility for the general public to inform itself. It sometimes happened that Emperor Franz I of Austria was mistaken for a

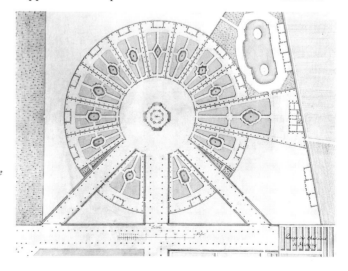

Ground-plan of the menagerie at Schönbrunn. Constructed after designs by Jean Nicolas Jadot in 1751/52, it formed the core of this historic zoo, and still exists today.

gardener by a visitor and asked for information, which he then knowlegeably dispensed. He also supervised his grandson, Napoleon's son, in his nature studies as the boy grew up at Schönbrunn, as a painting in the Memorial Room of the palace records.

Towards the close of the 18th century, the scientific and practical interest in nature was joined by a sentimental, romantic concept of nature which led to the creation of the »English« style of garden. Fortunately the gardens at Schönbrunn were not affected by this fashion because Emperor Joseph II, preferring the Augarten palace, did not live at Schönbrunn. His successor, Emperor Leopold II, reigned for too short a period to make his mark architecturally. The reign of his son, Emperor Franz II, was much longer in comparison, but was dominated by the Napoleonic wars which lasted nearly a quarter of a century. The financial resources were accordingly limited as the state constantly hovered on the edge of bankruptcy.

Since Emperor Franz was especially fond of the English type of garden, he had a large park laid out in this style at Laxenburg Palace. The gardens at Schönbrunn remained untouched.

White roe deer, porcupine and antelope in the imperial menagerie. Painting by the court animal painter Johann Georg Hamilton, 1724.

Napoleon's entry into Schönbrunn in 1809. Engraving by François Aubertin after a drawing by Alexander Delabarde.

Emperor Joseph II would have liked to have Schönbrunn boarded up - just as he had the Imperial Crypt at the Capuchin Church walled up - and he was deaf to all the representations of his building administrators urging repairs. The palace existed, it was the legacy of the great Empress, therefore it had to be preserved. It was shown to visiting nobility and royalty, the Emperor was proud of it, but it was not to be a source of expense. Eventually he had to allow the roof to be rebuilt since there was found to be rain damage in fifty of the rooms. His nephew Emperor Franz II was also continually confronted with the necessity for repairs and alterations in the construction of the roof. In the autumn of 1808 work was started, but pro-gressed only slowly, being halted again owing to the renewed campaign against France in 1809. The victorious Napoleon took up residence at Schönbrunn from May to October 1809. It was then that, enmity and contempt for the Emperor of the French notwithstanding, the Viennese court realised just how far the condition of the palace had deteriorated. The Congress of Vienna in 1813/14 brought the Habsburg palace into the lime-light once more. In the years 1817-19, when peace had finally returned, work was started on a complete replacement of the roof and the alteration of the garden façade according to the latest tastes. The court architect Johann Aman, a classicist of limited imagination, received the commission for the work. He altered the tall, arched windows on the second floor and simplified the entablature by continuing it in a straight line at the same height across the whole façade. The central projection was particularly affected by this. Aman also replaced the round clock which, integrated into the balustrade, had crowned the central section of the façade, with a horizontal clock, known as the Bird Clock. Emperor Franz II (who had officially dissolved the Empire in 1806 and as Franz I had borne the title of »Emperor of Austria« since 1804) was not especially pleased with Aman's consistent emphasis of the horizontal and thus corresponding alterations on the courtyard side were not carried out.

Inside the palace numerous but unspectacular renovations were effected, some of which the visitor of today can still see. Many of the parquet floors were relaid and the wall hangings in some of the rooms were renewed or replaced with »Indian« wallpaper. The decoration of the Blue Chinese Salon dates from this time. Large sums of money had already been spent on the renovation of the furniture for the guests during the Congress of Vienna. The redisposition of some of the palace rooms by Emperor Franz, his son Ferdinand as well as Archduke Franz Karl and his wife, Archduchess Sophie, the future parents of Emperor Franz Joseph, also involved renovation work.

When one reads that Emperor Franz I began spending the summer again at Schönbrunn, it should not be assumed that the palace had once again become the imperial summer residence and that the times of Maria Theresa had returned. The style of government had changed radically since the reign of Joseph II. The ruler and the court spent several weeks or months of each year travelling and for obvious reasons preferred the warmer seasons for this.

They made regular visits to the numerous lands and cities of their huge empire. From the Netherlands to the Bukovina, from Bohemia to Dalmatia they travelled right across Europe. The seat of government was either the Hofburg or a carriage on the move! In addition to this there were the continual campaigns. The ruler often accompanied his troops right to the borders of his territory; several times he was forced to flee. Emperor Franz twice had to vacate Vienna in the face of Napoleon's advance and withdraw to Moravia or Hungary. Thus in the years up until the Congress of Vienna, the court did not spend an extended annual period at Schönbrunn in the summer. However, with the return of peace, this practice was resumed, albeit curtailed by the many journeys that had to be made. The imperial family had expanded considerably and thus Schönbrunn came to be occupied all the year round, not least by Napoleon's son, the young Duke of Reichstadt, who died here at the age of twenty-one in the summer of 1832.

Even at that time the palace was regarded as an historic monument which should not be altered in any way, and concern grew as how best to preserve it. Emperor Ferdinand, for example, set up a commission to examine which of the paintings were in need of restoration. Famous painters such as Joseph Führich, Leopold Kuppelwieser and Ferdinand Georg Waldmüller were consulted.

In 1854 several rooms were refurbished for the young imperial couple Franz Joseph and Elisabeth. The following years and decades saw almost continuous work as plumbing, wiring and sewerage systems were installed, since Franz Joseph had chosen Schönbrunn as his permanent residence, despite the fact that this entailed travelling to and from the Hofburg nearly every day.

Many renovations and improvements were made for the World Exhibition held in Vienna in 1873, and the guest apartments - known as the »Freudenappartements« (Apartments of Pleasure) - were refurbished. The Napoleon Room and the Gobelin Salon were decorated and furnished as they still are today with tapestries from the Netherlands. A few years later, in 1891, when apartments for Crown Prince Rudolf were being fitted out on the ground floor (work which continued despite his death), the murals by Johann Bergl which so delight today's visitor were discovered underneath the wall hangings.

The last great building project in the gardens was the Palm House, begun in 1880, a huge construction in iron which has dominated the western part of the gardens ever since. Having suffered serious damage in the war, it was not restored until the early nineties, but like the palace, is now also a monument of architectural history.

The eastern Terrace Cabinet belonging to the apartments of Emperor Franz Joseph's parents, furnished around 1860.

In the last few years of the 19th century, the last years of peace in Europe, Schönbrunn came to embody an increasingly rigid form of politics. Franz Joseph had outlived his generation and with little personal connection to the world outside stood

The Gobelin Salon, as it was once furnished in the francisco-josephinian style.

at the head of a state which many saw as anachronistic. Even the Emperor himself spoke of being »an anomaly in the world of today.«

After the suicide of Crown Prince Rudolf in 1889, the dynastic rules designated a nephew of the Emperor as heir to the crown. Archduke Franz Ferdinand differed from the Emperor on many political issues and did not attempt to resolve his differences with his uncle but merely waited for his hour to come. In anticipation of this, he formed a kind of shadow cabinet at his residence, the Belvedere in Vienna. Schönbrunn and Belvedere, these twin jewels of Austrian architecture, became political catchphrases. It ended in tragedy: the heir to the throne was murdered by Serbian nationalists in Sarajevo while on a journey of inspection. Urged on by his generals, the aged Emperor embarked on a war against Serbia which escalated into the First World War.

In the third year of the war, Franz Joseph died at Schönbrunn on 21st November 1916. Not long afterwards his multinational state passed away, undone by the fateful tensions of its multiplicity and diversity.

Following the defeat of Austria-Hungary in the First World War, Emperor Karl refused a seat in the government and the »German-Austrian« Republic was proclaimed. The government expropriated the Habsburg dynasty and banished the Emperor and his family from the country. An enormous »legacy« fell into the lap of the Republic. Extensive alterations were made at Schönbrunn, many parts of the palace rented out, large parts of the park built on or closed off. Many things were allowed to fall into disrepair, for example the playgrounds used by the imperial children with their antique apparatus, the beautiful fittings in the stables or the furniture in the servants' quarters. The summer riding school was integrated into the park and the old, smaller palm house rented out to a film production company.

Whereas Schönbrunn survived the First World War virtually unscathed, the palace, together with the park and its monuments as well as several adjacent buildings were badly damaged by aerial bombing during the Second World War. Much was irretrievably destroyed. On 21st February 1945, a total of 269 bombs fell on Schönbrunn.

The German princes, led by Emperor Wilhelm II, congratulate Emperor Franz Joseph at the jubilee marking the 60th year of his reign, at Schönbrunn in 1908. Painting by Franz von Matsch.

After a long and difficult period of reconstruction which was hindered by both a lack of materials and expertise as well as obstruction on the part of the occupying powers, the imperial apartments were gradually reopened to the public by 1950.

Schönbrunn, a major work of architecture, a monument to high culture and the setting for so many important historical events, has its own unmistakable identity. It presents itself as a unique mixture of the festive and the intimate, the urbane and the rural, which many people have also found characteristic of the Viennese style of life.

The following guide to the palace is intended to convey detailed information on the furnishings of the individual rooms and draw a vivid picture of the people who once lived here.

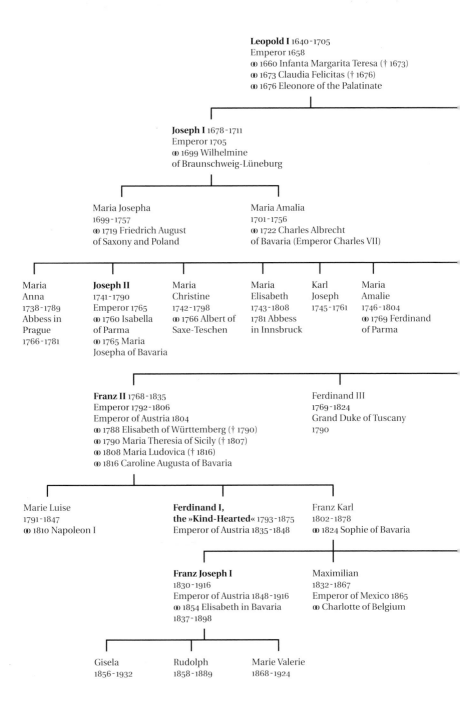

Leopold I 1640-1705
Emperor 1658
ⓧ 1660 Infanta Margarita Teresa († 1673)
ⓧ 1673 Claudia Felicitas († 1676)
ⓧ 1676 Eleonore of the Palatinate

Joseph I 1678-1711
Emperor 1705
ⓧ 1699 Wilhelmine
of Braunschweig-Lüneburg

Maria Josepha
1699-1757
ⓧ 1719 Friedrich August
of Saxony and Poland

Maria Amalia
1701-1756
ⓧ 1722 Charles Albrecht
of Bavaria (Emperor Charles VII)

Maria
Anna
1738-1789
Abbess in
Prague
1766-1781

Joseph II
1741-1790
Emperor 1765
ⓧ 1760 Isabella
of Parma
ⓧ 1765 Maria
Josepha of Bavaria

Maria
Christine
1742-1798
ⓧ 1766 Albert of
Saxe-Teschen

Maria
Elisabeth
1743-1808
1781 Abbess
in Innsbruck

Karl
Joseph
1745-1761

Maria
Amalie
1746-1804
ⓧ 1769 Ferdinand
of Parma

Franz II 1768-1835
Emperor 1792-1806
Emperor of Austria 1804
ⓧ 1788 Elisabeth of Württemberg († 1790)
ⓧ 1790 Maria Theresia of Sicily († 1807)
ⓧ 1808 Maria Ludovica († 1816)
ⓧ 1816 Caroline Augusta of Bavaria

Ferdinand III
1769-1824
Grand Duke of Tuscany
1790

Marie Luise
1791-1847
ⓧ 1810 Napoleon I

**Ferdinand I,
the»Kind-Hearted«** 1793-1875
Emperor of Austria 1835-1848

Franz Karl
1802-1878
ⓧ 1824 Sophie of Bavaria

Franz Joseph I
1830-1916
Emperor of Austria 1848-1916
ⓧ 1854 Elisabeth in Bavaria
1837-1898

Maximilian
1832-1867
Emperor of Mexico 1865
ⓧ Charlotte of Belgium

Gisela
1856-1932

Rudolph
1858-1889

Marie Valerie
1868-1924

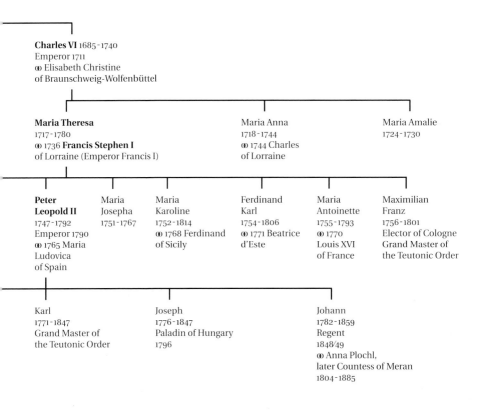

Charles VI 1685-1740
Emperor 1711
∞ Elisabeth Christine
of Braunschweig-Wolfenbüttel

Maria Theresa	Maria Anna	Maria Amalie
1717-1780	1718-1744	1724-1730
∞ 1736 **Francis Stephen I**	∞ 1744 Charles	
of Lorraine (Emperor Francis I)	of Lorraine	

Peter Leopold II	Maria Josepha	Maria Karoline	Ferdinand Karl	Maria Antoinette	Maximilian Franz
1747-1792	1751-1767	1752-1814	1754-1806	1755-1793	1756-1801
Emperor 1790		∞ 1768 Ferdinand	∞ 1771 Beatrice	∞ 1770	Elector of Cologne
∞ 1765 Maria		of Sicily	d'Este	Louis XVI	Grand Master of
Ludovica				of France	the Teutonic Order
of Spain					

Karl	Joseph	Johann
1771-1847	1776-1847	1782-1859
Grand Master of	Paladin of Hungary	Regent
the Teutonic Order	1796	1848/49
		∞ Anna Plochl,
		later Countess of Meran
		1804-1885

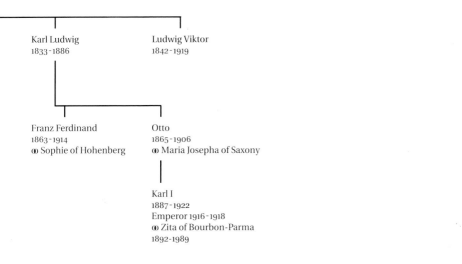

Karl Ludwig	Ludwig Viktor
1833-1886	1842-1919

Franz Ferdinand	Otto
1863-1914	1865-1906
∞ Sophie of Hohenberg	∞ Maria Josepha of Saxony

Karl I
1887-1922
Emperor 1916-1918
∞ Zita of Bourbon-Parma
1892-1989

The State Apartments

The state rooms and the gardens of the palace were open to the public at no charge when the court was not in residence from 1779, the year before Maria Theresa died. Today nearly all the rooms on the first floor and a number of rooms on the ground floor are open to Schönbrunn's visitors. Those on the ground floor include the Goess Apartments on the garden side of the east wing, which were decorated with the fanciful murals by Johann Wenzel Bergl and which are now generally known as the Bergl Rooms after him, as well as the palace chapel on the left-hand side of the courtyard side.

The first floor, the so-called *piano nobile*, contains the apartments of the Emperor, Empress and the imperial family, as well as the state rooms. Although they were used for different purposes over the course of the centuries, and often altered or refurnished, they still breathe the spirit of Maria Theresa's Vienna and its art, poised between the elegance of the Rococo and the restraint of Classicism. However, Schönbrunn is not simply the monument of a great ruler over the peoples of her lands; its name has a fixed place in the wider context of the history of politics; in it art and power combine to form an historic concept the significance of which is otherwise equalled only by Versailles.

The Blue Staircase

Entering the pillared hall on the ground floor we come to the staircase in the west wing which takes us to the first floor. The Blue Staircase was also used by Emperor Franz Joseph to reach his living quarters and study, as well as by diplomats and ministers of state on their way to deliver their reports or *Vortrag* (recitation) as it was called in the language of the Viennese court. It was used by not only by privy councillors, chamberlains, senior officials and officers on their way to audiences, but also by tens of thousands of people, fortunate or unfortunate subjects of the Emperor and King of Austria-Hungary, the largest European state after Russia.

The staircase derives its name from the predominant blue of the ceiling painting, which the Venetian artist Sebastiano Ricci executed between 1701 and 1703 for the dining room of the first palace built by Emperor Joseph I. The subject of the fresco is the glorification of the Emperor as a man of virtue and hero of war. The brief reign of Joseph I (1705-1711) was dominated by wars against France on the border of the Rhine, in the Netherlands and in Northern and Southern Italy. The hero is depicted in three different aspects: on one of the shorter sides he stands between a nymph and a satyr, exposed to the enticements of Venus. On the other side he is represented as the virtuous persecutor putting dissolute enemies to flight, and finally, striding upon a rising path of clouds, receiving the victor's crown of laurels before the throne of eternity.

Emperor Joseph I, who commissioned the original palace at Schönbrunn, portrayed as Roman-German Emperor wearing the coronation robes and imperial crown. The Crown of St. Stephen can be seen on the table.

The structuring of the walls, the frames of the doors and windows and the stucco decoration are also from the original building by Fischer von Erlach from 1695-1700. The rest is the result of the alterations carried out by Nikolaus Pacassi in 1743, with a few later additions, for example the balustrade. The bronze fittings were put up for the electric lighting around 1880. The most recent additions to the decoration are the two paintings on the landing, probably executed by the Dutch artist J. P. Bredael the Younger. They represent battle scenes from ancient history and myth. The two life-size figural groups in metal depicting two of Hercules' labours, which now stand in the entrance hall, once graced the dining room. They are hollow and were either vents for the warm air heating system or possibly (when filled with water) used for extinguishing torches. They are supposed to have come originally from the Belvedere palace, which became imperial property after Prince Eugene's death in 1738. Although the famous Dutch master Adrian de Vries has been proposed as their creator, this attribution is uncertain.

The first room one enters after the Blue Staircase is the billiard room. The billiard table was used by Emperor Franz I and was put here after his death in 1835.

However, the room is chiefly remarkable for the three large paintings commemorating the foundation of the Military Order of Maria Theresa and the jubilee celebrations one hundred years later. On 18th June 1757, Austrian troops under the command of Field Marshal Count Leopold Daun defeated King Frederick II of Prussia at Kolin (east of Prague), thereby destroying the latter's aura of invincibility. To commemorate this victory, Maria Theresa founded the first of her military orders of merit, the highest Austrian award for bravery for officers, to which she gave her own name. A painting by Martin van Meytens

depicts the ceremonial occasion when the order was awarded for the first time by Emperor Francis Stephen I, to Count Daun and Prince Alexander of Lorraine. A colourfully dressed group of courtiers can be seen gathered round the baldaquin in the Hall of Ceremonies in the Hofburg, but they do not seem especially interested in the patriotic ceremony.

One hundred years later, the significant achievements of the army, particularly during the course of the wars against Napoleon, could be looked back on with justifiable pride. Emperor Franz Joseph gave one banquet in the gardens for the officers of Vienna's garrison and another in the Great Gallery of the palace for the members of the order. Fritz l'Allemand recorded the festive events of this day in his two paintings, with the

Martin van Meytens and studio: First awarding of the Military Order of Maria Theresa on 7th March 1758 by Emperor Francis Stephen I.

Fritz l'Allemand: The centenary jubilee of the Military Order of Maria Theresa in 1857. Banquet given by Emperor Franz Joseph for the Knights of Theresa in the Great Gallery of Schönbrunn Palace.

handsome Austrian uniforms, the magnificent national costumes of the Hungarians and Croats as well as the elegant gala dress liveries of the lackeys.

The Walnut Tree Room

The adjacent corner room is known as the Walnut Tree Room, after the beautiful wooden panelling with which it was furnished in 1810. The carved and gilded wooden chandelier with forty-eight candles belonged to the original furnishings, while the white and gold stove was added in 1872. This room served as an audience chamber both for Emperor Joseph II and later on for Emperor Franz Joseph as well. The latter granted more than 250,000 audiences during the course of his long life! It was a Habsburg tradition, founded by the »People's Emperor« Joseph II, to grant an audience to any subject who so wished. In Franz Joseph's case, they were doubtless the reason for his wonderful memory for people.

The Emperor's writing desk has recently been set up in this room again. His personal set of writing implements, a green velvet folder with gold clasps, together with a number of sealed letters indicate the ruler's customary activity. The Emperor smoked cigarettes, but preferred Virginias, a type of cigar that was very popular at that time. A cigarette case with his monogramme also lies on the desk.

Another item from the original furnishings is the folding glass screen which was intended to protect against draughts. On the tables are two portrait busts, one of bisque porcelain portraying Archduke Franz Carl, and a larger one of his son, Emperor Franz Joseph.

Emperor Franz Joseph's Study

The room following the audience chamber is Emperor Franz Joseph's study. A painting by Franz von Matsch of 1915 records how it was furnished at the time, showing the conscientious ruler working by lamplight at his desk. Franz Joseph lived at Schönbrunn during the warmer seasons of the year and worked from the early morning onwards, receiving the reports of his ministers and officials and giving audiences in the adjacent room. At midday he often remained at his desk and had his luncheon brought to him on a silver tray which was set down beside the files, as related in the memoirs of Eugen Ketterl, his loyal valet of many years. Often at midday he would drive to the Hofburg, returning in the afternoon or evening. His elegant, black personal carriage, a small coupé, instantly recognisable from afar by its handsome horses and liveried coachman, was a familiar and fond sight to many Viennese which repeated itself day in, day out. The saying went that one could set one's watch by it.

The two portraits hanging today in the study were painted by Franz Russ in 1863.

Franz Russ:
Emperor Franz
Joseph in the full-
dress uniform of
an Austrian field
marshal in the so-
called German
service dress
version, with white
tunic and red
trousers. In the
imperial army a
distinction was
made between full-
dress and field
dress, as well as
between German
and Hungarian
colours.

The Empress wears a red cloak over a dress of white lace, the Emperor the full-dress uniform of an Austrian Field Marshal with the red and white ribbon of the Order of Maria Theresa.

A number of objects recall the imperial couple: two busts in bisque porcelain, a bronze statuette of Elisabeth, who was passionately fond

*Franz Russ:
Empress Elisabeth.
She wears a white
lace gown under
a red cloak together
with the famous
emerald parure
that had once
belonged to
Empress Maria
Theresa but had
been reset in 1810.*

of riding, and one of her richly decorated fans.

Behind the study were a cloak-room and a small kitchen.

The study and the following bedroom are also known as the »Emperor's Rooms«.

The Emperor's bedroom is notable for the plainness of its furnishings. The wall hangings are of brown rep, as is the upholstery of the chairs. The wash-stand with its marble top, the prayer-stool and the military-style iron bed were all obligatory items of furniture in the imperial bedrooms of the Hofburg and hunting lodges. The iron bed always proves to be of especial interest to visitors and supports the popular view of Franz Joseph's military lifestyle. It is said that he almost always wore uniform and that that his whole interest, or even his great love, was his army, with its hundreds of regiments and thousands of officers and soldiers. Even if this is too one-sided a view of his personality, the simplicity of this room bears witness to a sober, disciplined and conscientious attitude towards life which was bound to clash with that of the imaginative, sentimental, and above all egoistic character of the beautiful Empress Elisabeth, with her overriding zest for life.

Today fewer works of art grace the walls than during the Emperor's lifetime, since numerous portraits of his children and grandchildren which used to hang in this room have been transmitted through inheritance into private possession. The painting of the Virgin with Child and Saints is a copy after a work by Garofalo.

The portrait of the Emperor on his deathbed recalls the fact that Franz Joseph died here in this room on 21st November 1916.

On a console between the windows is a beautiful and very elaborate clock, crowned with a statuette of the Belvedere Apollo, a copy of the famous classical statue in the Vatican.

In 1899, an »English« lavatory was installed behind an invisible door between the bedroom and the following Terrace Cabinet.

From the western Terrace Cabinet (both this and its eastern counterpart were built by Pacassi around 1745), a door (normally kept locked) leads to the terrace above the colonnades which open the Parade Court to the Hietzinger Allee, a road leading out to the west. It was originally called the Altona or Altan Cabinet, and the terrace above the roof of the colonnade was glassed in.

This narrow room, which has beautiful silk wall hangings framed by gilded mouldings, is otherwise unfurnished except for a double portrait of the approximately eight-year-old Archduchess Maria Josepha and her four-year-old sister, Archduchess Maria Antonia (Antoinette), the youngest daughter of the Empress Maria Theresa. The French artist Pierre Benevault brought something of the French taste to the Viennese court with this work. He was aiming not so much at the individual characterisation of the two children, placing them rather in an impersonal, courtly setting, which was bound to displease an enthusiastic mother like Maria Theresa. She preferred the realistic portraits of her Swedish court painter Martin van Meytens, examples of which we will encounter in several of the other rooms in the palace, the first one in the next room.

Pierre Benevault: The Archduchesses Maria Josepha (b. 1751) and Maria Antonia (b. 1755). Benevault was summoned to Vienna as court painter and executed portraits of Empress Maria Theresa's children for the Belvedere Palace in 1759.

The first room, the windows of which face west and overlook the Kammergarten, is known as the Stairs Cabinet, and the adjacent room as the Dressing Room. We now enter the apartments of Empress Elisabeth. Brighter colours predominate here: for some parts, blue silk from Lyons was used for the wall hangings and curtains, and in others the colour scheme of the white and gold panelling and red brocade upholstery dating from the 18th century was retained. The atmosphere of the rooms is also characterised by the graceful pastel drawings, magnificent portraits of the imperial princesses, together with genre and landscape paintings.

Empress Elisabeth concerned herself much earlier than her husband with the installation of modern conveniences and comforts at the Hofburg as well as at the palaces of Schönbrunn and Laxenburg. Nonetheless, it was not until decades later, in 1880, that warm air heating systems, modern »English« lavatories, telephone lines and electric lighting were installed. Incidentally, the lighting was installed under the personal supervision of Thomas Alva Edison. By 1891 all the chandeliers at Schönbrunn blazed with the cold light of the age of technology.

From the Stairs Cabinet an iron spiral staircase leads down to the ground floor into a room opening out into the Kammergarten. Here there is a particularly striking portrait of three princesses at a tender age. They are three of Maria Theresa's older daughters: Maria Anna, Maria Christine and

Martin van Meytens: The Archduchesses Maria Anna (b. 1738), Maria Christine (b. 1742) and Maria Amalie (b. 1746).

Maria Amalia. Although they recline on silk, velvet and ermine, Meytens has successfully conveyed three unmistakeable little personalities.

At Schönbrunn, we will frequently encounter small wall cupboards or chests faced with lacquer panels from China or Japan. Precious objects from the Far East made of lacquer or porcelain were much admired in Europe and collectors were prepared to spend vast sums on acquiring them.

Portrait of an old man and a beggar woman by a Viennese artist who worked in the style of Jean Etienne Liotard, a painter whose works were especially favoured by Empress Maria Theresa.

The former dressing room of the Empress contains four pastel drawings by an unknown artist depicting simple folk in a somewhat idealised fashion: old people, a beggar, young girls in peasant costume. The predilection for pictures of this kind was widespread in the middle of the 18th century, the leading exponent of this genre being the Genevan artist Jean Etienne Liotard.

A few dark pieces of furniture from the second half of the 19th century - a wash-stand, mirror and a clothes stand - recall the former function of this room.

The Imperial Bedroom

In the bedroom of the Empress' apartments, which was the marital bedroom of the young couple, the over-ornate, almost pompous rosewood furniture forms a stark contrast with the blue silk wall-coverings. The furniture was intended to bear witness to the high standard of Viennese craftsmanship. According to an unconfirmed tradition, the Company of Viennese Cabinet-Makers gave it as a wedding present to the Emperor and Empress in 1854. It had special significance for Franz Joseph in that as a boy he had been trained as a cabinet-maker. Learning a manual trade had been a tradition in the Habsburg family for 400 years. The Emperors were not only »professional« rulers but also qualified cabinet-makers, wood-turners, watch-makers or goldsmiths. The lathe used by

Emperor Maximilian I at the end of the 15th century, for example, is preserved at Kreuzenstein Castle near Vienna.

To one side is a trolley with a swivel top which could be adjusted for height and swung over in order to serve breakfast in bed.

The painting of the Madonna above the double bed is a work by the Florentine artist Carlo Dolci and was part of the imperial paintings collection, as was Guido Reni's *Virgin and Child with the Young John the Baptist.*

On the wall at right angles to the window is a portrait of the Archduchess Maria Anna, the oldest daughter of Maria Theresa. We shall be hearing more about her later.

Guido Reni: Virgin and Child with the Young John the Baptist. The works of the Bolognese painter Guido Reni (1575-1642) and his followers - this Madonna could also be by G. A. Sirani (1610-1670) - corresponded to the emotional religiosity of the 19th century.

The walls of the white and gold salon of the Empress, which is flooded with light on sunny afternoons, were recovered with silk in 1873. The room is furnished with splendid pieces of furniture, among others a *chaise-longue* with a matching footstool and an occasional table, and contains a number of beautiful paintings. Two Italian landscapes by Philipp Hackert (1737-1807) depict the royal family of Naples helping with the grape and the corn harvest respectively. King Ferdinand IV was married to Maria Karolina and her children were thus Maria Theresa's grandchildren.

Philipp Hackert:
King Ferdinand IV
of Naples and Queen
Maria Carolina with
several of their
children at the corn
harvest. This type of
rustic idyll reflects
the aristocratic taste
for pastorals.

Philipp Hackert:
Two sons of King
Ferdinand IV of
Naples in rustic
costume at the
grape harvest.

The portraits in pastels of some of the
Empress' children were painted by an
Austrian artist around 1752 in the style
of Liotard, of whose work the Empress
was particularly fond. These include
the future Emperor Joseph II around
the age of eleven, his elder sister Maria
Anna and the next youngest children,
Maria Christine and Maria Elisabeth,
portrayed at the age of nine.

Joseph Kranzinger: Archduchess Maria Antonia around the age of 13. She is wearing a hunting costume and holds a riding crop in her right hand. The archduchesses also took part in court hunts. Elaborately-chased hunting guns belonging to Maria Antonia and her sisters have also been preserved.

On the shorter wall, next to the beautiful neo-Rococo stove, hangs a portrait of the Archduchess Maria Antonia, painted a little later around 1768. The future queen of France, Marie Antoinette, wears a fashionable hunting costume.

The personal guests whom Empress Elisabeth received in this salon came in through the Gardezimmer and a second intermediate antechamber which can be viewed briefly.

The Marie Antoinette Room

The large reception room of the Empress is known as the Marie Antoinette Room after a Gobelin tapestry which used to hang there. It was a gift from Emperor Napoleon III and depicted the French queen together with her three children as the artist Elisabeth Vigée-Le Brun had painted them in an official portrait in 1787.

Friedrich von Amerling: Emperor Franz I of Austria in the robes of the Order of the Golden Fleece.

The tapestry was replaced by a full-length portrait of Emperor Franz I of Austria by the Biedermeier artist Friedrich von Amerling. The first Emperor of Austria here wears the robes of the Order of the Golden Fleece, the most exclusive order in Europe. Founded as an order of Burgundian knights, it acquired power and reputation as the dynastic order of the Habsburgs. After the older

The Marie Antoinette Room

Empress died only two years after their marriage, Joseph becoming a widower for the second time.

The small portrait hanging beside the stove is of Archduchess Maria Leopoldina, who also suffered a tragic fate. Like her sister, Marie Louise, she was compelled to contract a political marriage. In 1817 she was married to the Brazilian Crown Prince Dom Pedro, to whom she was by far superior, both morally and intellectually. It was under her influence that Brazil asserted its independence from its mother country Portugal. Later on the marriage became extremely unhappy and Empress Leopoldine died in Rio in 1826 aged only 29 as the result of a miscarriage following physical maltreatment by her husband.

In later years Empress Elisabeth retired from official engagements and ceded the Marie Antoinette Room to her daughter, Marie Valerie. After the latter married, it was used from 1891 onwards as a reception room by Emperor Franz Joseph. It was here that the aged monarch received the official congratulations of all German sovereigns, headed by Emperor Wilhelm II, at the jubilee marking the 60th year of his reign. The scene was recorded in a painting by Franz von Matsch, now in the Historische Museum der Stadt Wien.

Spanish line of the Habsburgs died out, the German line assumed sovereignty over the order and still retains it today. Part of the treasure of the order is to be found in the Secular Treasury of the Vienna Hofburg.

On his dark red, gold-embroidered velvet robe the Emperor wears the combined stars of the Grand Crosses of the Austrian orders of merit: the Military Order of Maria Theresa, the Hungarian Order of St. Stephen, the Austrian Order of Leopold and the Order of the Iron Crown, which Emperor Franz had founded in honour of the Italian provinces joined in the Kingdom of Lombardy-Venetia.

Around his neck is the golden chain of the order, from which the symbol of the order, the golden ram's fleece, is suspended. This indicates membership of the order but is not a medal of merit or other decoration.

The small pictures in this room portray children of Maria Theresa and were painted by her busy court painter Martin van Meytens and his studio.

Portraits of Joseph II and his second wife, Maria Josepha of Bavaria, hang on the shorter walls of the room, next to the windows. The unpopular

The Nursery

The first nursery is also known as the Blue Salon of Archduchess Marie Valerie's Apartments. The harmonious contrast between the white and gold panelling and the blue curtains and upholstery (an ensemble which bears witness to the refined taste of the imperial court around 1854), forms the setting for a series of charming portraits. An unknown Austrian painter known for want of any other name as the »Master of the Archduchesses' Portraits«, executed these likenesses of the six surviving daughters of Maria Theresa around 1767/68. They are not portraits of children, but of grown-up princesses - even the twelve-year-old Maria Antonia is already a young lady.

The oldest child, Maria Anna (her portrait hangs to the right of the door to the Breakfast Room), was born when her mother was still an Archduchess and was her mother's much-loved problem child. Frequently ill, she devoted herself not only to reading and »artistic« activities such as drawing, embroidery and amateur dramatics, which were taught to and expected of the Empress' daughters, but also collected coins and botanical specimens. She was thus following the example of her father, whom she adored and whose favourite she was. Shortly before this portrait was painted she became the abbess of the Noble Order of Gentlewomen in Prague, but mostly remained in Vienna while her mother was still alive. She died in Klagenfurt.

*Archduchess
Maria Christine
(1742-1798) at the
age of approxi-
mately 25, shortly
after her marriage
to Duke
Albert of Saxony.*

Maria Christine, whose portrait hangs on the opposite wall, next to the mirror, was the only daughter allowed to marry for love, albeit not her first choice and not until after her father the Emperor's death.

Together with her husband, Duke Albert of Saxony, she shared in the foundation of an important collection of drawings and graphic art, today famous all over the world as the Albertina. She herself drew and painted competently. Some of her works may be seen at Schönbrunn.

Maria Elisabeth (her portrait hangs next to that of Maria Anna) was as beautiful as she was coquettish and was a much-prized trophy in the marriage stakes; the kings of Poland, Spain and France were all candidates for her hand. In 1767 she was dis-figured by smallpox and subsequently remained a spinster. She became abbess of the Noble Order of Gentle-women in Hall in Tyrol.

Maria Amalia had to marry Duke Ferdinand of Parma, who was five years younger than herself, in 1769. She was the only child who removed herself entirely from the influence of her mother.

Maria Karolina holds a leaf of paper bearing a portrait of her father, indicating her artistic inclinations. She was, however, unable to devote herself to them for long, as she had to marry King Ferdinand IV of Naples in place of her sister, Maria Josepha, immediately after the latter's death. Ferdinand was uncouth, un-educated and ugly (*il re lazzarone*), but was either of such good judgement or so indolent that he left the business of governing to his energetic wife. Maria Karolina resembled her mother in her qualities of cleverness, bravery and loyalty. In the park at Schönbrunn she had a monument erected at the spot where she had had a little garden as a child.

Maria Antonia, the youngest of the daughters, was transplanted at the age of fifteen from the warmth of the family at Schönbrunn to the luxurious and profligate court of Versailles. For a few all too carefree years, the beauty of the Crown Princess Marie Antoin-ette, already evident in the portrait in

Archduchess Maria Antonia (1755-1793), later Queen of France, at the age of 12.

Archduchess Maria Carolina (1752-1814), shortly before her marriage to King Ferdinand of Naples and Sicily.

the Blue Salon, held triumphant sway. Responsibility and depth of character came to her too late as queen, but during her imprisonment and at her death on the guillotine she proved herself a true daughter of her great mother.

Beneath Marie Antoinette's portrait stands a rare and beautiful piece of rosewood furniture which was once in her possession. It is fitted with bronze-gilt mounts and embellished with gouache painting under glass and fine reliefs of bisque porcelain from the factory at Sèvres. This secretaire or bureau was made by the famous cabinet-maker Adam Weisweiler around 1780. It came to Empress Charlotte as a gift from Emperor Napoleon II and Empress Eugenie. Charlotte was the wife of Maximilian of Mexico, the unfortunate brother of Franz Joseph.

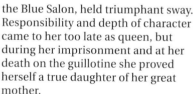

The cabinet on the southwest corner was probably used by Empress Maria Josepha, Joseph II's second wife, as a breakfast room. Before this it had been panelled in green and had belonged to the apartments of Emperor Francis Stephen and Maria Theresa, possibly being used for the same purpose. The framed appliqué embroidery was executed by Maria Theresa herself, probably together with her daughters. The decoration of this room, like that of the Porcelain Cabinet in the east wing, is an example of the personal collaboration of the imperial family in the decoration of the palace rooms.

Also characteristic of the Maria Theresian taste are the Chinese porcelain vases above the mirror and the two large green standing vases. Together with the old rose curtains and upholstery they strike a harmonious chord which makes this little room unforgettable.

The Yellow Salon, so called after its Louis Seize furniture, was once the bedroom of Emperor Francis Stephen and Maria Theresa in the early years of their marriage until 1747. Later it was occupied by the Emperor's sister, Charlotte of Lorraine, and it is mentioned as having been used by Emperor Franz I as his study. At that time the walls were covered with »Indian paper«, but this was replaced by wooden panelling in 1854. Today the walls are hung with pastel drawings by Jean Etienne Liotard which were probably all from the possession of Maria Theresa. She loved the work of this flamboyant painter from Geneva. He paid three visits to Vienna, in 1742/3, 1762 and 1778, portraying the young Empress and later the imperial couple together with their flourishing brood of children. He also brought other works with him which Maria Theresa then bought. Some she hung

*Jean Etienne
Liotard: Children
with soap bubbles.*

in her private apartments at Schönbrunn while others were put into the
imperial paintings gallery. The little
girl with a doll is taken to be Liotard's
daughter, Marie Françoise.

On top of a console decorated
with intarsia stands a magnificent
Parisian clock which also indicates the
phases of the moon. It is said that it
was a gift made by Napoleon to his
father-in-law, Emperor Franz I of
Austria. However, this story, which
smacks a little too much of tour guide
inventiveness, cannot be confirmed.

The Balcony Room was the bedroom of Archduchess Marie Valerie, the youngest daughter of Emperor Franz Joseph and Empress Elisabeth. Her mother was extremely fond of her and the two women were very close, the daughter often accompanying her mother on her journeys abroad until her marriage to Archduke Franz Salvator from the Tuscan line of the Habsburg dynasty in 1890. After the death of the Empress, the Arch-duchess also assumed official duties

at the side of her father.

In the Balcony Room there hangs a painting by Martin van Meytens depicting the three elder sons of Maria Theresa. Joseph (in the centre), Karl Joseph (right) and Peter Leopold (left) are dressed in military uniforms despite their tender age. As sons of the Emperor they were each made commander-in-chief of a regiment at an early age. Joseph had commanded a Dragoons regiment since his eighth year; his uniform is, however, adapted to conform to the traditional rules governing courtly dress. As the second oldest son, Karl Joseph was commander-in-chief of a Hungarian regiment for political reasons and thus wears its picturesque uniform with all the characteristics of the Hungarian national dress. The youngest son appears as a little cuirassier.

On the side walls are a portraits of eight of Maria Theresa's children. On the left are the three oldest daughters, Maria Anna, Maria Christine and Maria Elisabeth, together with her youngest child, Maximilian Franz, who later became Archbishop and Elector of Cologne and sent the young Beethoven to study with Haydn in Vienna. On the opposite wall are the sisters Maria Karolina and Johanna Gabriele, who died at an early age, as well as their brothers Ferdinand Karl and Peter Leopold, the »cuirassier«.

The uniform white and gold-painted wooden panelling and the stucco ornamentation which seems to flow out from the corners of the Mirror Room, its white marble fireplaces and the twelve bronze-gilt girandolas (chandeliers) correspond to Pacassi's plan for a remodelling of the Baroque palace in Rococo taste. The basic colour scheme is enlivened by seats upholstered in red called tabourets as well as oriental standing and table vases of blue-and-white porcelain. Like the preceding rooms, the Mirror

Room was used for various functions over the centuries. Joseph I used this as his bedroom; after its refurbishment it became an audience chamber or dining room for »lesser occasions«. One such occasion was the memorable reception given to Leopold Mozart and his children, the eleven-year-old Nannerl and the six-year-old Wolferl. On 13th October 1762, here in the Mirror Room, he played to the Empress on the harpsichord, »*sprang up onto her lap, threw his arms around her neck and promptly covered her face with kisses*«. The proud father then goes on to relate: »*In short, we were with her from three to six o'clock, and the Emperor himself came out of the other room to fetch me that I might hear the Infanta play upon the violin...*«

In a recess with doors in this room there is a small altar with a painting of the Madonna by Agricola. It was in front of this altar that newly-appointed ministers were sworn in, probably from the late 18th century onwards but certainly before the reign of Emperor Franz Joseph.

The Rosa Rooms

The three Rosa Rooms bear the name of the painter Joseph Rosa, who came from a German-Dutch family of artists by the name of Roos and worked at the courts of Dresden and Vienna before being permanently appointed by Emperor Joseph II as director of the imperial paintings gallery in 1772. Between 1760 and 1765, for the three state rooms on the garden side of the palace, he executed a series of fifteen mountainous landscapes showing peasants working in the fields, shepherds and their flocks resting by the banks of a river or travellers on a journey. Expressed in these paintings is an early romantic enthusiasm for nature which Maria Theresa shared with the artist, as well as an interest in dynastic history, for one of the paintings in the large Rosa Room shows the ruins of Habsburg Castle, the original castle of the dynasty, situated in the Aargau in Switzerland (next to the door to the Mirror Room).

Martin van Meytens: Empress Maria Theresa, aged approximately 25, when she was intensively occupied with the remodelling and decoration of Schönbrunn Palace. The Empress is here portrayed as Queen of Hungary. She wears a gold-embroidered ceremonial gown and holds the sceptre of the Kings of Hungary. On the table beside her is the Hungarian crown of St. Stephen.

Joseph Rosa: Mountainous landscape with the ruins of Habsburg Castle. Not only the atmosphere of the picture but also the fact that Maria Theresa had commissioned a painting of the castle where her dynasty had originated from indicate an early Romantic sensibility and an interest in personal history, attitudes which did not become widespread until the early 19th century.

Joseph Rosa: Mountainous landscape with travellers resting and a laden donkey.

Joseph Rosa: Herd of goats and sheep with a sheep dog in the foreground.

The Lantern Room

From the third Rosa Room a door leads directly into the Round Chinese Cabinet. It is kept closed in order to keep the climatic conditions in this precious room as stable as possible. We can thus only view this room and its counterpart, the Oval Cabinet, from the Small Gallery. We now proceed to the Lantern Room, a large antechamber, which can also be entered from the Blue Staircase. Its name perhaps derives from the lackeys who used to stand here ready to light the guests to their carriages. It was in any case the main entrance to the reception rooms in the centre of the palace, to which we will now turn our attention.

The Great and Small Galleries

These two magnificent rooms are the centrepiece of the alterations that Maria Theresa commissioned from Pacassi. They could be used in a wide variety of different ways.

The Great Gallery was the banqueting hall and ballroom, but generally large numbers of people assembled here to be conducted through the antechambers on both sides, i.e. the Lantern Room and the Carousel Room, to an audience with the Emperor. General public audiences were held on Sundays and private audiences on Fridays, while ministers and high-ranking officers came to present their reports daily.

The Great Gallery is the most impressive room created in the epoch of Maria Theresa. Forty metres long and ten metres wide and high, it is spanned by a shallow-vaulted ceiling covered in frescoes executed by Gregorio Guglielmi in 1760-62. These represent in a most unusual way the contemporary political, military and economic situation of the »Austrian Monarchy«, that is, the Habsburg lands in their entirety. The fresco in the large central section shows the Austrian Crownlands, represented by allegorical figures, gathering to pay homage to the ruling couple, who are rendered quite naturally, in their patriarchal role, i.e. not allegorically. The crowns of Hungarian and Bohemia, the Austrian Archducal hat together with other symbols of power are being presented to Maria Theresa.

The works of peace: the promotion of art and science. Fresco by Gregorio Guglielmi on the ceiling of the Great Gallery, 1761.

The two lateral frescoes set Austria as depicted in the central section between those two force fields which have always determined the weal and woe of a state and its people: between the powers of peace, in which commerce, agriculture and trade flourish, and the powers of war.

The scenes of war are illustrations of contemporary events taking place in the Seven Years' War (1756-1763) against Prussia, which was then drawing to a close: generals in conference, marching troops, grenadiers opening fire - everything is rendered with convincing immediacy.

The walls of the Great Gallery are structured by mighty Corinthian pilasters bearing a shimmering tracery of golden lines, sprays of leaves, flowers and artfully combined implements, weapons and musical instruments which eventually supports the framework of the ceiling frescoes. This magnificently elaborate stucco work was executed by Albert Bolla at the same time as Gregorio Guglielmi was painting the ceiling frescoes. It had to be thoroughly restored in 1870 after the lighting was adapted for electricity. The large wooden chandeliers are

*Maria Theresa,
Queen of Hungary
and Bohemia,
Archduchess of
Austria.
Detail from the
central fresco by
Gregorio Guglielmi
on the ceiling
of the Great Gallery,
1761.*

*Emperor Francis
Stephen I, husband
of Maria Theresa.
Marble bust
by Balthasar Moll,
1765.*

The Great and Small Galleries

Queen Marie Antoinette of France, youngest daughter of Maria Theresa. Marble bust with medallions showing children's portraits around the edge of the socle. By Charles van Poucke, 1779.

first mentioned in 1858, and bear a total of 1,104 bulbs which illuminate this magnificent room, the shimmering white and gold brightness of which is heightened and expanded by the huge crystal mirrors.

The Small Gallery was the setting for family celebrations such as the name-days of the children and their parents, intimate musical soirées and small social gatherings. This room is less lavishly appointed, the decoration being composed on a lighter, more delicate note. The structuring of the walls flows into the cornicing and the vaulting of the ceiling.

The ceiling painting in the Small Gallery celebrates the »benevolent rule« of the »Empress«, who as Queen of Hungary, Bohemia, Dalmatia, Croatia, Archduchess of Austria, Duchess of Styria, Carinthia, Carniola and numerous other lands, Grand Princess of Siebenbürgen and Margravine of Moravia and Istria etc., etc., in fact ruled her lands in an assured and responsible manner. She bore the title of Empress solely as the spouse of the Emperor.

At Schönbrunn, however, she was the great wife and mother, despite the fact that she never let politics out of her sight. Appropriately enough, the shorter sides of both the Galleries have portraits with particular family connections. On one side of the Great Gallery is a lively Baroque marble bust by the Austrian sculptor Balthasar Moll. It represents Emperor Francis Stephen, who although he remained in the background politically, was very much the head of the family for the simple reason that he meant so much to Maria Theresa.

On the other side is a Classicistic work by J. Cerachi, a bust of Emperor Franz II, the last »Roman« and first Austrian Emperor. He was the Empress' first grandson and his arrival was joyfully celebrated.

In the Small Gallery beside the doors to the Chinese Cabinets are busts of two of Maria Theresa's daughters. They stand on identical socles which are faced with red porphyry and decorated with oval medallions of marble bearing likenesses of children. Next to the door to the Oval Cabinet is a bust of Queen Marie Antoinette of France dated 1776.

The Chinese Cabinets

The early 18th century had an especial predilection for lacquerwork, silk wall hangings and porcelain from China and Japan. At Schönbrunn there are a large number of these precious artefacts which graced many a princely residence. Some of them were incorporated into cabinet pieces by Viennese craftsmen. Vases, figurines and ornaments of porcelain, as well as folding screens containing painted lacquer panels, are to be found all over the palace. Two rooms which are decorated and furnished according to European notions of the Orient are to be found on both sides of the Small Gallery in the curvature of the central projection of the palace. These are the two Chinese Cabinets, the Oval Cabinet on the western side and the smaller Round Cabinet on the eastern side.

The white wooden panelling known as *boiserie* contains large mirrors and black and gold lacquer panels of different shapes and sizes, on which are painted landscapes, branches covered in blossom or animals. Small consoles grow out of their gilt frames, supporting items of blue-and-white porcelain. The ceiling of the cabinet is a shallow dome which is framed by an elaborate frieze. Rocailles are joined to undulating scrolls and flowery tendrils. Peacocks, rare birds, butterflies and oriental vessels underscore the exoticism of the room. Large blue and red porcelain vases from Japan together with upholstered and painted seats called tabourets stand on the elaborate parquet flooring which, like the chandeliers, was made in Vienna.

Both cabinets served as conference rooms. Secret staircases led up to them and the Oval Cabinet had a kind of dumb waiter so that talks could be held without risk of being disturbed or spied upon. A table laden with food and drink and supposedly drawn up through a secret opening in the floor was known as the »Table of Conspi-

racy«. After these conferences, the Empress liked to remain behind and play cards, for example lansquenet or faro, the latter carrying considerable risks for her; the Empress played for high stakes and often lost, a habit which came in for criticism from her husband, who was economical by nature. He administered her private fortune and was not pleased when she was forced to run up debts with him.

The Carousel Room

Leaving the magnificent architectonic space of the Gallery in an easterly direction we come upon the Carousel Room. This was Emperor Francis Stephen's »first *anticamera*« and until the 19th century it remained a typical antechamber with no less than six doors. It was not until 1864 that two of them were bricked up and the walls hung with paintings which are also of interest to today's visitor. In the painting on the right-hand side we can see splendidly-dressed lords and ladies mounted on horseback or riding in small, elaborately carved Rococo carriages in the Winter Riding School of the Vienna Hofburg. As the young queen of Hungary and Bohemia, Maria Theresa had rather fancifully celebrated the reconquest of Prague by the Austrians on 3rd January 1743, which proved to be the turning point in the War of Silesia against Prussia and Bavaria. Maria Theresa leads a mounted quadrille, while eight other women riding in delicate harnessed carriages with cavaliers at the reins drive up the riding arena.

Martin van Meytens: The inauguration of the Royal Hungarian Order of St. Stephen and the first awarding of the order by Queen Maria Theresa.

Martin van Meytens and studio: Ladies' Carousel at the Viennese Court in the Winter Riding School of the Hofburg, 3rd January 1743. One of these carved wooden carriages has survived and is displayed in the Wagenburg.

For Maria Theresa, the election and coronation of her son Joseph as German-Roman King in 1764 was a political event of the utmost importance in that it secured the succession to the imperial title for the Habsburg-Lorraine dynasty. Emperor Francis Stephen in fact died unexpectedly the following year and Joseph II assumed the reins of government in the Empire.

On the occasion of Joseph's coronation, Maria Theresa founded the monarchy's first civil order of merit. She named it the Order of St Stephen, after the patron saint of Hungary, and gave it the traditional form of organisation as an association of equal and like-minded men with statutes, functionaries and formal robes, which were naturally in the Hungarian national colours of red, white and green.

Executed by Meytens' workshop, the painting depicts the first ceremonial award of the order on 6th May 1764. As Queen of Hungary, Maria Theresa is awarding the Grand Cross to four men. Emperor Francis Stephen is permitted to watch the proceedings incognito, since Hungary did not belong to the Holy Roman Empire and he thus had no official function at this ceremony.

Next to the door leading out of the Carousel Room hangs an impressive full-length portrait of Emperor Charles VI, Maria Theresa's father. In his youth he had been King of Spain, and was moreover a highly musical man and also commissioned many architectural projects. Here, however, clothed in a Spanish coat-dress of gold brocade and decorated with the Order of the Golden Fleece, he appears as the Holy Roman Emperor, the highest-ranking ruler in Europe.

On the small table benath the painting is a display cabinet containing a recently acquired bust of Charles VI which is notable for the strength of its artistic expression.

The Hall of Ceremonies

Martin van Meytens and studio: The entry into Vienna of Princess Isabella of Parma as the bride of the future Emperor Joseph II on 6th October 1760. The procession of carriages is making its way towards the Augustinerkirche. In the background are the Imperial Library, the Winter Riding School and, at the extreme right, the old Hofburg theatre.

The paintings in the Hall of Ceremonies also record a highly political event in the guise of splendid festivities. The diplomatic skills of the State Chancellor, Prince Kaunitz, had brought France onto Austria's side. This new political constellation in Europe demanded that the future emperor Joseph, who had just turned eighteen, should take a wife from the French Bourbon dynasty. The choice fell on Princess Isabella of Parma, who was of the same age. The grand wedding held in October 1760 is depicted in five paintings hung in this room after Maria Theresa's death.

The largest of the paintings sets the bride's arrival against an imaginary backdrop of buildings along the Augustinerstrasse. On the extreme right in front of the Hofburg, one of the two triumphal gates is visible; the other stands in the space that the artist Meytens needed to depict the arrival of 94 six-horse carriages, a number confirmed by contemporary newspaper reports. The silver and blue coach of the bride is escorted by the imperial Swiss guards in black and yellow uniforms.

Beside this huge painting an open door affords access to one of the oratories of the palace chapel. Let us take this opportunity to take a brief look inside. (A description follows on p. 150)

Martin van Meytens and studio: Banquet at court on the occasion of the marriage of Isabella of Parma.

Martin van Meytens and studio: The marriage of Joseph (II) and Isabella of Parma in the Augustiner-kirche on 6th October 1760.

Further paintings in the cycle show the wedding in the Augustinerkirche, the wedding feast, the evening »*souper*« and a dramatic performance in the great Redoutensaal (ballroom) of the Hofburg.

Even at the time of their execution (1762/1763) these paintings caused a sensation on account of their size and faithful reproduction of detail. This is true of the rendering of the buildings, the people and their clothing, the dinner service etc. But did the artists in Meytens' studio also let their imaginations run loose somewhat? This would seem to be the case if the small figure in the theatre painting (next to the exit) is really meant to be the young Mozart. The child prodigy was certainly not present, but his name had been on everybody's lips since his performance at Schönbrunn in October 1762.

Placed among this cycle of paintings is the most famous of all the portraits of Maria Theresa. It was Emperor Franz Joseph who first had it hung here in place of a baldaquin. The »First Lady of Europe« wears an exquisite gown of Mechlin lace. On the table lie the crowns of Hungary and Bohemia with which she was crowned and, as a symbol of her highest dignity, the imperial crown, the insignum of her husband, Francis Stephen I. When he was elected and crowned Emperor in 1745, people said: »*The husband of the Queen of Hungary has become the German Emperor.*«

The massive size of the paintings should not distract the visitor's attention from the beautiful stucco work in the Hall of Ceremonies. It represents symbols of martial victory - palm branches, standards, various types of weapon, a marshal's baton - which are bound together by garlands and which partly hang down free into the room. The stately, ceremonial character of the room is conveyed with a light hand.

The Hall of Ceremonies, which measures approximately 13 x 14 metres, served principally as the antechamber to Emperor Francis Stephen's apartments. Here the imperial family gathered before entering the oratories of the palace chapel. However, it was also used for large celebrations such as chris-tenings, name-days and birthdays, as well as for the court banquets which followed all individual audiences. For these occasions gala dress was *de*

rigueur and this meant even more elaborate ceremony than normal: those attending were seated according to the strictest order of precedence and the lackeys wore gala livery. Maria Theresa disliked this sort of formality at Schönbrunn, as she considered it inappropriate for a household living »in the country«, where things should be less formal than at the Hofburg. Neither was the Emperor a friend of excessive formality. And yet even the audience granted to the Mozarts demanded a gala day! In general, ceremony and etiquette were gradually simplified during the epoch of Maria Theresa. Thus Emperor Francis

Stephen, for instance, permitted uniform to be worn at audiences; he himself sometimes even wore uniform instead of the Spanish coat-dress.

He no longer ate at a separate table as Emperor Charles VI had done, but together with 12 to 16 people at his table. The second table was considerably larger, being mostly laid for 30 to 60 people.

One of the doors in the Hall of Ceremonies affords a view of the Equestrian Room. On view is the so-called Marshal's Table, which was laid each day for the senior court officials and high-ranking officers when the Emperor was in residence at Schönbrunn. On the walls hang numerous equestrian paintings by Johann Georg Hamilton, painted around 1720 for Emperor Charles VI. They are in fact »portraits« of the Emperor's favourite horses and form a unique ensemble.

They are grouped around a large painting by Philipp Ferdinand Hamilton and Martin Rausch depicting a *battue*, a type of hunt on horseback, in the water meadows of the River March to the east of Vienna, with Emperor Joseph I, who commissioned Schönbrunn, at the centre of the painting. The picture was, however, painted many years after Joseph I's death.

The important role played by the horse as the companion of the »hero« - long years of experience went into its breeding at the court studs, it was carefully broken and then trained at the imperial riding schools - has already been touched upon. Whether as war horse or parade-horse, it was indispensable. During the 18th century, riding developed as the

amusement of the landed gentry and in the 19th century became the neck-breaking sport of the aristocratic world, compulsory for the officer class. Emperor Franz Joseph, as an officer, was a superb and elegant horseman even in his later years. Empress Elisabeth was an athletic horsewoman par excellence and without doubt one of the best of her time, even taking part in extremely hazardous steeplechases in England.

Hunting had also been the preserve of princes since the Middle Ages. It was a privilege hated by the peasants both because their crops suffered from damage caused by game and because the game could have provided a much-needed source of food. It also entailed a tiresome compulsory service to be rendered by

Johann Georg Hamilton: Paintings (in fact portraits) of horses from the imperial studs. Hamilton was court animal painter to Emperor Charles VI. His paintings were executed on copper panels which resulted in a remarkably smooth and glossy surface. The horses ridden personally by the Emperor had names which indicate their Spanish-Neapolitan bloodlines: Brillant, Hermoso, Diamante, Sincero, Valido, Curioso.

hunt-servants and beaters. Emperor Franz Joseph was a passionate sportsman; however, with his son Crown Prince Rudolf and his nephew Archduke Franz Ferdinand, later heir to the throne, this passion verged on the pathological.

Schönbrunn was witness not only to Maria Theresa's times of happiness but also to her times of misfortune. For her, for whom the family was the basis of all political and artistic endeavours, the death of her beloved husband was inevitably a devastating blow. »*I have lost the kindest of all men*«, she wrote to her friend Countess Enzenberg, »*he was my one and only consolation in life.*« The imperial

court had travelled to Innsbruck in August 1765 in order to celebrate the marriage of Archduke Peter Leopold to the Spanish Infanta Maria Ludovica. During this sojourn, the Emperor died suddenly in the Innsbruck Hofburg in the arms of his son Joseph, coincidentally in the same room in which he had been born 57 years previously. His successor as head of the Empire, Emperor Joseph II as he was from then on, inherited not only this venerable title, to which little actual power was attached, but also Francis Stephen's large personal fortune. As co-regent with his mother, he gained increasing influence in the Hereditary Lands of the Habsburgs (which were by then already known as the Austrian Monarchy), familiarising himself with the problems that he hoped to or was later to solve. Emperor Francis Stephen I had also been Grand Duke of Tuscany. This important title was not to fall to Austria, and so the next oldest brother, Peter Leopold, succeeded to this title. As a result, the newly-wedded couple travelled straight to Florence in order to take up the reins of power.

At Schönbrunn, Maria Theresa began to remodel the *retirada*, the private apartments of her late husband. It was at this time that the rooms of the east wing that adjoin the Hall of Ceremonies received their present appearance. For this Maria Theresa engaged not only architects, cabinet-makers and leading artists, but also purchased costly lacquer panels and had other precious materials which had previously been used in other parts of the palace incorporated here. This suite of rooms situated in the east wing contains the most important achievements of Viennese interior decoration of this era together with exquisite masterpieces of Viennese cabinet-making.

The Hall of Ceremonies adjoins the Blue or Chinese Salon. It was at one time the Emperor's audience room or council-chamber. What it looked like at that time is unknown. Maria Theresa had the walls panelled in walnut and decorated with stucco work which lacks the lightness of the Rococo, already displaying distinct Classicistic features. The Chinese wallpaper which gives the room its name was hung at the beginning of the 18th century. Each length of wallpaper has three motifs arranged in vertical order: an oval and a rectangular blue panel with everyday Chinese scenes, surmounted by a basket of flowers; birds, butterflies and flowers are scattered over the light-coloured background. The furniture is exquisite: chests faced with panels of Far Eastern lacquer and tables with tops of Florentine *pietra dura*. The chairs were upholstered in blue silk in 1857. It was in this room, on 11th November 1918, that Emperor Karl I renounced any share in the affairs of state, an action that was ultimately tantamount to his abdication.

The Vieux-Laque Room

The Vieux-Laque Room derives its name from the oriental lacquer panels which are set into dark-brown walnut panelling embellished with carvings by Johann Georg Leithner. The ceiling, too, lives up to the name of the room with its ornate decoration of gilded stucco work into which small lacquer panels have again been inserted. This magnificent room, remarkable for its stylistic homogeneity, was remodelled after the designs of the French architect Isidor Canevale, shortly after the panels had been purchased for the sum of 12,869 gulden. The splendid, lavishly decorated furniture was not put here until some time during the reign of Emperor Franz Joseph, but corresponds stylistically to the interior decoration of the room. The Rococo is drawing to a close, the playful lightness of the Chinese Cabinets has given way to heavy, dark solemnity. The parquet floor, though it harmonises perfectly with the decoration and furnishings, was not laid until around 1872.

Anton von Maron: Grand Duchess Maria Ludovica with her children Maria Theresia, Franz (who later became emperor) and Ferdinand, who succeeded his father Peter Leopold as Grand Duke of Tuscany. On the table is a bust of Maria Theresa, the children's grandmother.

Set into the walls are three family portraits, which Maria Theresa commissioned from Pompeo Batoni and Anton von Maron, two famous painters active at the time in Rome. The expressive portrait of her husband, Emperor Francis Stephen, who points to a statue of Justice, was executed by Batoni in Rome in 1772, (i.e. after the Emperor's death). It is flanked by a double portrait of his two highly-gifted sons: Joseph, who was astute, sardonic and yet easily hurt, and Peter Leopold, who had an equable and diplomatic temperament, and by a portrait of the Empress' daughter-in-law Maria Ludovica with her three eldest children. One of these is the first

grandson, Franz, who was born in Florence in 1768.

The impressive double portrait of Emperor Joseph II and his brother was painted by Batoni in Rome in 1769. The young emperor was staying in the Eternal City at that time in order to exert his influence on the papal election. The portrait conveys not only his lucid intellect but also his impatience and obstinacy, traits which often led to his large-scale reforms only being accepted under duress or even failing entirely. Grand Duke »Pietro Leopoldo« on the other hand was an outstanding ruler, famed and admired for his wise reforms and clever policies. Within the family, he played the role of merciless critic of

the court in Vienna, objectively
assessing the tense relationship
between Maria Theresa and Joseph.
When he succeeded his childless
brother as Emperor and Lord of the
Habsburg Lands, he had the difficult
task of mitigating or repealing many
of the former's harsh and over-hasty
reforms. Maria Theresa was so taken
with the portrait of her two highly-
gifted sons that she asked the artist to
paint a copy of it. This today hangs in
the Kunsthistorische Museum.

The following room is kown as the Napoleon Room. Napoleon conquered Vienna twice. The first time was in 1805, allied with Bavaria and Württemberg in his campaign against Austria and Russia which he sucessfully concluded with the victory at Austerlitz and the Peace of Pressburg, and the second time in 1809, when Austria fought on her own against France. The successful struggle for liberation in Tyrol and the sensational victory achieved by Archduke Karl over Napoleon at Aspern had no ultimate influence on the outcome of the war. Napoleon had already taken Vienna in May and was residing at Schönbrunn, the Viennese court having fled to Hungary. In autumn 1809 the Peace of Schönbrunn was signed and in the following March the marriage of Napoleon to Archduchess Marie Louise, the daughter of Emperor Franz, was to consolidate the peace in Europe.

Scenes from military life. These tapestries were woven in Brussels in the 18th century but the designs are in the style of Netherlandish painting from the time of the 30 Years' War.

It is probable that the Napoleon Room served as the great Corsican's bedroom during both his stays in Vienna, a brief one in 1805 and one of almost six months in 1809. No authentic accounts of this period have survived. However, Napoleon's son, living in Vienna as the Duke of Reichstadt, chose this room as his sitting room and died here in 1832.

In October 1809, during a parade in the Parade Court at Schönbrunn, a pastor's son fron Naumberg made an assassination attempt on Napoleon. It failed and the assassin paid for his patriotic deed with his life.

The so-called Napoleon Room was Maria Theresa's bedroom in the first years of her marriage, and also the room where some of her children were born. Since 1873, this room has been hung with Brussels tapestries after

designs by Hyacinthe de la Peigne
(Scenes from Military Life). The
portrait of Emperor Francis Stephen I
by Maron is a companion piece to the
paintings in the Vieux-Laque Room.
The Emperor wears the Order of the
Golden Fleece and the red and white
ribbon of the Grand Cross of the
Military Order of Maria Theresa.

The floor of the Napoleon Room,
as in a number of other rooms in this
wing, was relaid in 1947 following
bomb damage in the Second World
War.

The Porcelain Room takes its name from the carved wooden framework of the white painted wooden walls, which is painted blue and white in imitation of porcelain. A particularly charming feature is provided by the crossed parasols, the handles of which are tied together with bows. The panelling contains blue ink drawings, arranged in a strict vertical pattern. These were executed by Emperor Francis Stephen and two of his daughters in 1763 after French models. The decoration of this original room, which signals the end of the Rococo and the beginning of Classicism, was designed by Isabella of Parma, the wife of Crown Prince Joseph. Four medallions portray the three »imperial artists« and Archduke Albert of Saxony, husband of Archduchess Marie Christine. The ceiling is decorated with blue-tinted stucco work.

The artistic decoration of this small room is the most striking example of the personal part played by the imperial family in the furnishings and decoration of the palace. This did not merely involve the allegorical representation of the familiar virtues of the ruler and the glorification of dynastic history or the ostentatious display of power and riches as in a hundred other European palaces. Schönbrunn exemplifies the ideal of the family that the »first and universal mother« of the Empire had set her heart on.

The chandelier was made in the Vienna porcelain factory and the porcelain clock in Meissen.

Probably the most famous room in the palace is the »Millions« Room on the west front. The shimmering splendour of the wooden panelling and the precious Indonesian miniatures gave the room its name. After the death of her husband, Maria Theresa had this wooden panelling transferred here from the Upper Belvedere. Documents after 1767 mention a »Vicatin Cabinet« that was used as a conference room. The word »vicatin« is an archaic term for a type of tropical rosewood. Here it is structured by a shimmering golden network into vertical panels, most of which contain three rocaille frames. The beauty of this meticulously carved ornamentation reveals itself only after concentrated examination. The doors and fireplace as well as the mirrors, which are placed directly opposite one another, are all integrated into this play of golden tracery in a virtuoso manner. Beneath one of the mirrors, where one would usually find a fireplace or a table, stands a mock French chest of drawers.

The portrait bust in porcelain represents Marie Antoinette. It is a work by J. R. Lemoyne and exists in several versions. One of these is in the Kunsthistorische Museum in Vienna, another in Paris.

Scenes from the life of a Moghul ruler. Above: Battle scene with war elephants; below: a noble rider with his retinue. Miniatures with gouache and gold leaf on vellum.

The miniatures, 81 leaves in all, depict scenes from the life of rulers and grandees of the Mogul Empire in the 16th and 17th centuries. Rembrandt himself knew of these miniatures. They were cut down to size arbitrarily and put into the frames without any kind of thematic coherence.

The decoration is continued above the cornicing in wooden imitations;

the lattice work is painted and frames
lively wall paintings executed to
match the miniatures.

The wooden panelling of this
room was removed for the duration of
the Second World War and stored in
Salzburg. When the situation had
returned to normal, the separate
pieces were fitted back onto the walls
like an intricate jigsaw puzzle.

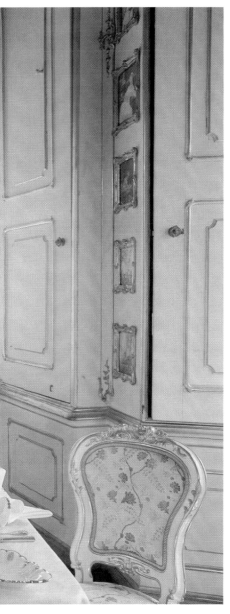

From the Millions Room we can look into the Miniatures Cabinet in which a small table is laid ready for breakfast. In this corner room we can see the wall which would normally be hidden from view reflected in a mirror. This wall is decorated with 57 small framed watercolours, all copies of Dutch or Italian paintings executed by Emperor Francis Stephen and his daughters Maria Anna, Maria Christine and Maria Antonia.

Proceeding along the eastern side of the palace we come to the Gobelin Salon. Since the Renaissance, woven hangings had been appreciated as a versatile wall decoration, and wall tapestries were a standard item of furnishing in any princely palace of the Baroque. The most important factories of the 16th and 17th centuries were in the Low Countries. However, in the second half of the 17th century the Gobelin factory in Paris became so important that since that time all woven wall hangings have been loosely and incorrectly referred to as »Gobelins«, including those that have hung in this large room on the east side of Schönbrunn Palace since 1873. Like those in the Napoleon Room, these are in fact Brussels tapestries from the 18th century. They depict scenes with peasants, fishermen and mariners. The six armchairs are upholstered with small tapestries depicting light-hearted genre scenes which together represent the twelve months of the year. The designs for these charming scenes were made after paintings by the Dutch artist David Teniers the Younger, who had been court painter to the Habsburgs in Brussels.

The Gobelin Salon is the first room of the apartments formerly belonging to Archduke Franz Karl and Archduchess Sophie, the parents of Emperor Franz Joseph, and was used by them as a drawing-room. Following the death of his mother in 1872, the Emperor had the rather plainly furnished apartments of his parents redecorated, during the course of which these tapestries were hung here.

It is unclear when the large and elaborate folding screen made of eight Japanese lacquer panels was placed in this room. It could have been in 1873,

for a new wave of enthusiasm for the Orient had begun sweeping Europe around this time. Artists such as Toulouse Lautrec or Van Gogh also fell under its spell.

The adjoining Breakfast Room of Archduchess Sophie also derives its name from its last occupiers, the parents of Franz Joseph. Like the Red Salon which follows, it was also at times used as a library. Today it is furnished as the Memorial Room of the Duke of Reichstadt and contains paintings of the latter both as a child at work in his garden and on his deathbed. After the defeat and abdication of his father, Napoleon, the two-year-old Napoleon Franz, who bore the title of »Roi de Rome« nominally became Napoleon II, but he went into exile with his mother, Marie Louise, in Vienna. Here he grew up at the court of his Austrian grandfather while his mother led her own life as

Set into the wall between the two windows of the Memorial Room is a full-length portrait of Emperor Francis Stephen wearing the uniform of his regiment, which he had commanded as hereditary prince of Lorraine and had then taken over into imperial service. After that time it was always commanded by the reigning emperor and it existed as the 1st »Emperor« infantry regiment until 1918.

The Memorial Room

Grand Duchess of Parma. The boy first bore the title of »Prince de Parme«, but after 1818 assumed the title of Duke of Reichstadt (in Northern Bohemia). His name in the family was simply »Fränzchen«. Numerous objects, brought by his mother to Vienna, recall his life: his sumptuous cradle in the Imperial Treasury, his little perambulator in the Wagenburg, his portrait and sword in the Museum of Military History. The prince's upbringing followed the traditional Habsburg pattern, with the little boy being required to study botany and work in the garden, as recorded by the painting executed by the artist Carl von Sales. Fränzchen's much-loved companion was a little crested lark which was stuffed after its death and is here displayed in a glass cage. It came from the estate of Count Johann Foresti, a learned gentleman from Trento, who had assumed the education of the four-year-old prince and was his tactful companion until the boy reached the age of nineteen.

On 22nd May 1832, the young prince died at Schönbrunn, in the same bed his father supposedly used to sleep in. His early death spared him the strains of a life spent as pretender to the French throne.

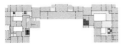

Once furnished with library bookcases and tables, the Red Salon today contains a number of portraits. Immediately to the right as one enters is a portrait by Meytens of Joseph II in a Spanish dress-coat, the traditional and only permissible court dress, which this emperor later abolished. With the imperial crown beside him, he holds the sceptre in his left hand, which indicates that he was already Roman King (1764) or even Emperor (1765). The ribbon is that of the Order of St. Stephen.

Emperor Leopold II, who briefly (1790-1792) succeeded his brother Joseph II after ruling over the Grand Duchy of Tuscany in an exemplary fashion for 25 years, is shown in the robes of the Order of the Golden Fleece. With his right hand he points to the imperial insignia.

Emperor Franz Joseph was portrayed
by Engelmann in the robes of the
same order, while a portrait painted
some thirty years earlier (1850) by
Anton Einsle shows him in the
uniform of an Austrian Field Marshal.

The Terrace Cabinet

The eastern Terrace Cabinet, like its counterpart on the west front, lies above the colonnade at the corner of the Parade Court. The fresco of floral bouquets was painted around 1770 by the otherwise little-known artist Johann Zagelmann.

The painted *trompe-l'oeil* architecture towards the ceiling of the room opens up to reveal a blue sky, in which putti playfully pelt each other with flowers.

The Bedchamber

The bedroom of the Franz Karl apartments, the windows of which look out onto the Parade Court, was the room where Franz Joseph was born. »The Emperor's Birthday«, the 18th August, was for nearly seven decades a public holiday celebrated throughout the huge empire. Franz Joseph mostly celebrated it in his beloved Bad Ischl, where he went every summer to hunt. When Archduke Franz Joseph was born at Schönbrunn, the palace was still part of the village of Hietzing, far outside the city, situated on the banks of the River Wien which were not yet built up at that time. The room where he was born, which had been a bedroom since the 18th century, was refurnished as such for the Maria Theresa Exhibition in 1980. The large state bed, probably made in 1736 after designs by Claude Lefort Duplessis, together with the matching wall hangings, belonged to the furnishings of the bedchamber of Maria Theresa in the Hofburg. As the name indicates, it served not for nightly repose but for purposes of ceremony. After completing her morning toilette, the Empress would slip into the state bed in order to hold an audience or to display herself in the role of proud mother with one of her newborn infants.

Two paintings by Martin van Meytens portray the two eldest sons of Maria Theresa. On the left is the serious, reserved Joseph, the future emperor, and on the right the charming Karl Joseph, who died of smallpox in 1761 at the age of 16, deeply mourned by his parents and the whole court.

The Study

In the adjoining study belonging to Archduke Franz Karl hang several paintings of interest. On the wall by the windows there are a number of smaller pictures, nearly all of which were executed by Archduchess Maria Christine. She based her likenesses of her parents, her grandmother Empress Christine (Maria Theresa's mother) and her brothers and sisters on large-scale portraits, some of which we have already encountered elsewhere in the palace. Two of her family scenes have proved especially popular: the imperial family at the giving of presents on St. Nicholas' Day and the depiction of Joseph II at the lying-in of his wife Isabella (1762).

The giving of presents in the imperial family on the Feast of St. Nicholas. Archduchess Maria Christine painted this picture after a contemporary engraving by Jacobus Houbraken after a work by C. Troost. The Archduchess also based her picture of Emperor Joseph II at the lying-in of his beloved first wife Isabella on a work by C. Troost.

Archduchess Maria Christine: Self-portrait at the spinning-wheel.

In the 18th century it was the custom on the feast of St. Nicholas to give children presents or to punish them by not giving them any. At Christmas there were neither Christmas tree nor presents, it being a purely religious, ecclesiastical festival.

The little picture of the imperial family celebrating St. Nicholas in a very uncourtly fashion was painted by Maria Christine after a Dutch engraving. The furniture and clothes are therefore meant as a joke and are not to be taken literally. The portly father and the purposeful mother certainly do not represent what is generally thought of as Their Roman-Imperial Majesties, who in public were constrained by a ceremonial which allowed them neither a free step nor an informal word. On the extreme left

the artist has portrayed herself threatening her brother Ferdinand with a rod. Maria Antonia happily displays her new doll, while the youngest, Maximilian Franz, is enjoying some gingerbread under the table.

The painter of all these pictures and many others in the palace also executed a self-portrait. She shows herself sitting at her spinning wheel in the Miniatures Cabinet, surrounded by her own works.

Martin van Meytens: Emperor Francis Stephen I and Maria Theresa surrounded by their family, c. 1754/55.

The most important work in this room in artistic and historical terms is the well-known portrait of the imperial family by Meytens. Emperor Francis Stephen I and Maria Theresa are surrounded by their large family. The artist has chosen as a setting an imaginary terrace in the palace which opens out like a stage set into a view over the Parade Court. The painting must have been executed around 1754/55, when eleven children were alive, shortly after the birth of Ferdinand Karl in June 1754, who lies in a little cot surrounded by four of his sisters. Joseph, the thirteen-year-old Crown Prince, clothed in red and gold court dress, stands at the centre of the star in the marble floor, turned towards his mother, who wears a dress of blue silk atlas. Beside her stand the two middle sons, Carl Joseph, in the uniform of his Hungarian regiment, and further towards the back, Peter Leopold. Next to the father, who is dressed in a Spanish coat-dress of gold brocade, stand the two eldest daughters, the sixteen-year-old Maria Anna and the twelve-year-old Maria Christine. Maria Elisabeth, the third-oldest daughter, looks out between Joseph and the Empress. Maria Antonia and Maximilian Franz had not yet been born and three children had already died.

Finally, there are two portraits of women who played an important role in Maria Theresa's life. To the right of the door hangs a portrait of the Empress' mother, Elisabeth Christine. She is portrayed as the widow of Emperor Charles VI. Born in Wolfen-büttel, the princess married Charles in 1708 when he was King of Spain, the wedding therefore taking place in Barcelona. Politically gifted, she acted as Stadholder and »Captain-General« when Charles had to hurry back to Vienna on the death of his older brother Joseph I. Elisabeth Christine and Charles had a happy marriage, although it was not blessed with children until many years later in Vienna. Elisabeth had four children, of whom two daughters lived to adulthood. The long, vain wait for a male heir cast shadows over her life. She survived Emperor Charles VI by ten years, but the beautiful, light-hearted »white Lizzy«, famed for her pale complexion, had become a corpulent woman who suffered from depression.

To the left of the door is a portrait of Countess Maria Caroline Fuchs. She was the nursemaid, governess and bosom friend of the young Arch-duchess. The portrait, which shows her as a widow, was painted around 1730. After Maria Theresa's marriage, she became the Keeper of the Empress' Household and confidante of both husband and wife. The Emperor used to while away the evenings in the company of his sister, Charlotte of Lorraine, and Countess Fuchs when Maria Theresa retired early in order to be able to begin the affairs of government early in the morning. (Her court officials usually had to start work at 7 am!)

When the countess died in 1754, as a mark of affection and gratitude, the Empress decreed that she should be interred in the Crypt of the Capuchin Church, the only person to be buried there who was not a member of the Habsburg dynasty.

The Corner Salon

In the large salon at the corner of the palace we may only take a look at three large-scale portraits, masterpieces by the court painter Martin van Meytens.

On the left is Archduchess Maria Anna in a pink dress with a fashionable hooped skirt. Opposite her is Joseph II's second wife, the beautiful Isabella of Parma, wearing a blue dress. The sisters-in-law were twenty-five and twenty-two years old respectively.

On the pilaster between the windows, towards the perron, hangs a double portrait of the eight-year-old Maria Christine and her brother Peter Leopold, who was five years younger. The girl's tiny lapdog is a papillon, a breed which was extremely fashionable at that time. The crown in the background is the Austrian archducal hat.

This attractive painting is one of the many double and group portraits of Maria Theresa's children to be seen at Schönbrunn. The children are dressed as adults; the girls in laced bodices, décolletage and elaborate jewellery, the boys in powdered wigs with swords at their sides. One can hardly tell their age. However, this »fancy dress« corresponded to the reality of court ceremonial!

The Palace Chapel on the Ground Floor

Consecrated to St. Mary Magdalene, the palace chapel is largely unchanged from when it was built as part of the first palace by Fischer von Erlach. By 1728 it was not only finished in its construction but also completely decorated and furnished, probably after designs by Andrea Pozzo. After 1740, Maria Theresa had the portal moved and the oratories and galleries which were accessible from the Hall of Ceremonies altered and their number increased. By 1744 the interior decoration had also been renewed. The Empress had paintings by Daniel Gran put up on the ceiling and the altarpiece by Johann Michael Rothmayr (*The Vision of St. Mary Magdalene*, today in the Augustinerkirche) replaced with a painting by Paul Troger *(The Betrothal of Mary)*. Georg Raphael Donner designed the marble altar and executed the relief for the tabernacle. The latter's pupil, Franz Kohl, supplied a new retable for the altar and the frame for the painting. Kohl was also responsible for the lead-gilt statues representing John the Baptist and a Mater Dolorosa. A few days after Maria Theresa, together with her family (still small as yet) and the court entourage had removed to Schönbrunn on 20th April 1745 to spend the summer there for the first time, the Archbishop of Vienna, Count Sigimund Kollonitsch, reconsecrated the palace chapel. The solemnities lasted four hours (from 8 am to 12 pm) and were followed by a banquet. At a number of places, the path to the chapel was covered with planks where construction work was still going on, a fact which contributed to make the atmosphere less constrained than usual without the customary disputes as to rank and precedence.

Emperor Franz I of Austria had a wooden crucifix, an outstanding work of art executed by the Swabian sculptor Leonhard Kern in 1625, hung in the palace chapel. This was, however, removed to the Ecclesiastical Treasury of the Hofburg in 1986.

In 1984 the old organ case was enlarged to accommodate a larger modern organ. During the course of these alterations, the galleries were restored to how they looked during Maria Theresa's reign.

The Bergl Rooms on the Ground Floor

A strange, exotic world awaits us in
these rooms. Walls and ceiling are
covered in landscape painting which
conveys the illusion of a remote world
alive with exotic birds and animals.
Here nature is not untouched but
ordered according to human notions.

In the gardens of the palace, nature is ordered according to architectonic principles, and in the Botanical Garden according to scientific and pedagogical aims. In the Bergl Rooms it is structured into a painted garden architecture by balustrades, arbours and Rococo vases. The visitor's eye is led past these into the gardens of splendid villas or temples.

Johann Wenzel Bergl's rendering of the plants and fruits is based on studies of nature, which he could easily have made in the hothouses of the palace gardens. He could also have sought advice from the botanists belonging to the circle around Emperor Francis Stephen as he brought the world of the tropics into the chilly rooms of the ground floor. In

Gardens, hothouses with figs and oranges, an apothecary's garden and the menagerie. At Schönbrunn the Emperor was able to realise all of these projects. He summoned scientists and horticulturalists, mostly from Holland, where floriculture had achieved world fame. The system of classification of plants according to Linnaeus had also started its triumphal march from Holland and the botanical cultivations at Schönbrunn were accordingly named the »Dutch Garden«. The most important of the scientists in Vienna was Nicolaus Joseph von Jacquin. Commissioned by the Emperor, he undertook an expedition to the West Indies and South America between 1755-59 and brought back extensive collections of

her old age, Maria Theresa used these rooms as her »summer rooms« when it became too hot and oppressive in her apartments upstairs.

This collaboration between artists and scientists, painting and botany, was brought about and especially encouraged by Emperor Francis Stephen.

Like many other princes who were influenced by the philosophical-pedagogical movement originating in France, he devoted himself to scientific collections which included live specimens from nature: the Botanical

plants and stuffed animal specimens. The colourful illustrations contained in his scientific reports of the expedition could have served as models for Johann Bergl as he and his assistant Martin Steinrücker decorated eight of the rooms in the the east wing and three rooms in the west wing of the ground floor with their illusionistic murals between 1769 and 1777.

The carved wooden chandeliers with flowers and fruit and the highly original gilded stove in the form of a tree trunk originated at the same time as Bergl's work.

The following generation covered over the murals with grey canvas screens. It was not until 1891 that these were removed, and in 1965 restoration work was started on the murals and measures undertaken to eradicate the damp. Today four rooms in the east wing are open to the public.

Since the east and southeast Bergl Rooms were occupied by Crown Prince Rudolf and the south Bergl Rooms (those that are on view) by Countess Marie Goëss, Keeper of the Empress' Elisabeth's Household, they are also known after these personages as the Crown Prince and Goëss Apartments respectively.

The Palace Theatre

»We must have theatrical performances - without them one cannot remain in such a large residence.« This utterance of Maria Theresa's expresses her unbounded enthusiasm for the theatre. She loved music and dance, she had a beautiful voice and enjoyed singing, even in front of foreign guests, and was thus very much a part of the tradition of both her own family and the city of Vienna. Vienna had been a centre of music theatre since the 17th century. The Habsburg rulers of the German branch of the dynasty were respected composers in their own right, for example the emperors Ferdinand III, Leopold I and Joseph I. They kept orchestras and opera ensembles as well as engaging famous poets, artists and musicians at the Viennese court. The writers, composers, stage designers and even the singers were almost exclusively Italians - Vienna was as it were the musical capital of Italy! Italian was the language of the imperial court and the second language of the city.

Emperor Charles VI had inherited the great musical gifts of his father, Leopold I, putting on performances of operas himself and conducting them when he was not sitting in the orchestra pit among the musicians. Taught by Johann Joseph Fux, he summoned Antonio Caldera to Vienna, endeavoured to engage Vivaldi and Goldoni and employed two other Italians as court poets: first the Venetian Apostolo Zeno (1688-1750) and from 1729 onwards the Roman Pietro Antonio Metastasio (1698-1782), who had until then been active in Naples, ruled at that time by Austria.

Although Metastasio had difficulty in accustoming himself to the »*formality of court life*« and the »*clamorous splendour*« that prevailed at the court of »*the most sublime personages on Earth*«, he stayed in Vienna until the end of his life. Metastasio possessed a serene attitude to life, devoting himself to Beauty and Virtue, an attitude that corresponded to Maria Theresa's enlightened rule. He was thus the antithesis of the frivolous and liberal French theatre. He wrote lyrical poems or canzonas, together with numerous libretti for operas and operettas, as short sung works were still called in those days, as well as ballets. The composers of his time regarded his libretti as particularly poetic and musical. Metastasio's opera libretti were set to music by Caldara, Wagenseil, Gluck, Haydn and Mozart, and Gluck considered the text so important that he once wrote: »*The poet executes the drawing, the composer merely colours it in.*« Metastasio also formed the musical taste of the Emperor's two daughters, Maria Theresa and Maria Anna. He became the favourite poet of the Empress and contributed to the numerous festivities held at Schönbrunn.

Besides the theatres in the city there were also stages in the imperial palaces. At Schönbrunn members of the imperial family and court put on small-scale theatrical performances in the Hall of Ceremonies or in the Small Gallery. The theatre was an important part of culture: it was not only entertainment but also outward show, regarded not only as something to be passively admired but to be participated in enthusiastically. Professional troupes were engaged to perform in the orangery which was empty during the summer months.

At Maria Theresa's wish, Nikolaus Pacassi built a theatre during the years 1743-1747 at the north-west corner of the Parade Court, where there had previously been stables and coach houses. Due to the length of the period spent by the court at Schönbrunn it became not only the most important of all palace theatres but played a not unimportant role in the history of the opera.

The repertoire included opera, operetta, ballet and Italian or French comedies. When the imperial offspring put on a performance, for example as a surprise for their father or mother on their name-day, improvisations often took place in the palace. The grown-up archduchesses performed in small operas, conducted by their brothers Joseph or Peter Leopold from the harsichord. Their admiring mother would then sit in the first row of the stalls with the rest of her children and not in the central loge.

In 1767 the opera *Alceste* by Christoph Willibald von Gluck was given its first performance here. It was the second of his great »reform« operas. The performances were not open to the general public. The rules of court ceremonial or the Schönbrunn house rules dictated by the Empress to her Lord High Marshal determined who was permitted to attend. The programme of the theatre was decided by the »Director-General of Spectacles«. This office was long occupied by Count Franz Wolf Orsini-Rosenberg, who played an important role in the lives of Mozart and Salieri, twin rivals for the favour of the court, since he ultimately decided who would receive the commission for a new opera.

In 1767, Maria Theresa (with the complete agreement of Joseph II) decided to have the palace theatre altered and enlarged. There were a number of reasons for this: an increased need for a suitable setting for official functions, an intensified interest in classical French tragedy and - albeit still somewhat tentative - in German literature. Ferdinand von Hohenberg designed and built the new theatre, whereby the original charm of the Rococo interior and its »marble and stucco splendour« was lost.

In the new theatre Mozart was present at a performance of *Alceste* in 1781 and several of his own operas were premiered here. In 1786, when one of these premieres took place as part of a grand reception given by Jospeh II, the palace theatre proved to be too small and the festivities had to be transferred to the Orangery at Schönbrunn. The programme included Mozart's *Impresario* and Salieri's *Prima la musica e poi le parole*.

Napoleon, who was a keen theatregoer, commanded numerous performances of very different programmes at the palace theatre during his sojourns at Schönbrunn. The French Emperor was an impatient man, and long works had to be shortened for him, or sometimes only one act would be performed, followed by a ballet. In 1805 the famous Italian composer Luigi Cherubini gave a concert here. Since Napoleon had to rely on Viennese actors for dramatic performances, bizarre linguistic confusions occasionally arose: in 1809 Racine's *Phaedra* was performed, but in the German translation by Schiller, while Napoleon read the French original.

In the following decades the ensemble of the Burgtheater regularly appeared at the palace theatre. Their performances during the World Exhibition of 1873 acquired especial fame, above all because of the prominent figures from politics and nobility present in the audience. In 1896 electric lighting was installed and other alterations undertaken to adapt the palace theatre to the demands of modern performances.

After the First World War, the palace theatre was used as a subsidiary stage by the Burgtheater and in 1929 Max Reinhardt opened his Acting Seminar here.

After the Second World War, the public performances of the Reinhardt Seminar were staged here together with the summer festival of the Vienna Chamber Opera. Further alterations became necessary to bring the theatre up to the standards of modern stage technology as well as to fulfil security requirements. These were completed in 1980.

Our times have discovered a new, atmospheric setting for dramatic performances at Schönbrunn: for the last few years operas have been performed on summer evenings in front of the backdrop of the Roman Ruins, to great acclamation from audiences.

The Palace Gardens

The Palace Gardens

As we leave the palace behind us and enter the parterre of the gardens, what immediately strikes us is the expanse and symmetry of the grounds that spread out before us, together with the way the main axis dominates the whole design. Approximately 200 metres long, this central path begins with the driveway under the palace and leads to the large fountain at the foot of the hill.

Above this as the main optical focus rises the Gloriette, which is also a belvedere, i.e. a vantage point from which one may enjoy the panoramic view that Fischer von Erlach had intended for the first projected palace.

Through the avenues which lead diagonally away to the left and right we see the sculptures belonging to two pools. These lie on the intersection of the diagonals with the second of the three continuous avenues running at right angles to the main axis, known as the Lime Avenue.

The diagonal running in a westerly direction is the Zoo Avenue with the star-shaped basin which originally lay in front of the perron of the palace, as can be seen in Bellotto's painting. The sculpture which is reflected in the water is probably the most famous of the Schönbrunn nymphs.

Johann Christian Wilhelm Beyer: Naiad in the Round Basin, with a view of the Obelisk.

To the east our eyes are drawn to the naiad in the round pool which Hohenberg designed as a symmetrical counterpart to the star-shaped basin.

The significance of the gardens as a part of the palace and its grounds and the phenomenon of the interpenetration of nature and architecture in the Baroque garden has already been discussed in the introduction to this guide.

The state of the gardens and the distribution of the sculptures and buildings as they appear today do not present a homogeneous picture. Work on the gardens was started in 1765 to new designs by and under the personal supervision of the architect Ferdinand von Hohenberg, but it went on for over a decade and was not completed until the end of the 1770s after several changes in the plans. Thus the gardens, which had already suffered a transformation from Baroque to Rococo, ended up with several Classicistic elements as well.

A competition was held to decide who would design the sculptures for the park. The resulting commission was won by Johann Christian Wilhelm Beyer, a sculptor from Gotha. Beyer was an artist of considerable gifts. After spending years in Italy, he was active at the porcelain factory in Ludwigsburg and had come to Vienna in 1769. For this large-scale commission he engaged more than a dozen assistants from 1773 onwards, who together - albeit with varying talent - created the sculptures of classical gods and heros which today people the parterre or are half-concealed in the ornamental shrubberies and arbours. Beyer, who received the honorary title of »Court Statuarius«, had the task of completing the commission within three years.

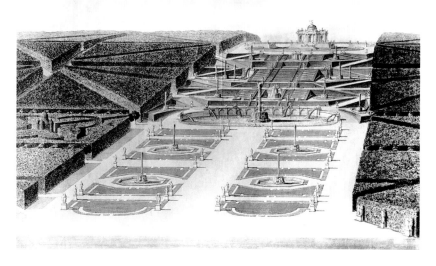

He executed approximately half the statues himself and made models for the rest, relying heavily on the porcelain figurines he had made in Ludwigshafen. Few of his assistants can be regarded as artists in their own right. They were allowed to chose the simpler models to copy and received from Beyer the sum of 1,000 gulden for one statue. Beyer himself received 1,200 gulden for an individual statue and 2,000-3,000 gulden for a group, and thus became a rich man!

All the statues are the same height and were made at the marble quarry in Sterzing. They represent mythological or historical figures.

This description of the statues begins at the left-hand (eastern) corner of the palace, at the so-called Crown Prince Garden. We will proceed along the clipped avenues of lime, chestnut and sycamore which form a green foil for the white marble of the statues. The statues facing one another have similar compositions and are thematically linked. The old numbering appears on the right-hand side of the socle.

1   Queen Artemisia grieving over the urn of her husband Mausolus. The sculptor Johann Baptist Hagenauer allegedly gave her the facial features of Maria Theresa (by Hagenauer and Jakob Christoph Schletterer);

2   Calliope, the muse of epic poetry, with a scroll and double flute, popularly called »The Piper« (by Johann Christian Wilhelm Beyer);

3   Junius Brutus swearing revenge beside the lifeless body of Lucretia (by Ignaz Platzer);

4   Bacchus and Ceres, the gods of wine and the cultivation of cereals and, like their opposite numbers (Janus and Bellona), allegories of war and peace (by Günther);

5   Aeneas rescuing his father from the flames of Troy (by Johann Ferdinand Prokop);

6   Angerona, the goddess of discretion (by Beyer);

7   Jason with the Golden Fleece (by Beyer);

8   Aspasia, the learned wife of Pericles (by Beyer);

9   Omphale, Queen of Lydia, with the lion's skin and cloak of Hercules; the statue of Hercules stands opposite (by Joseph Anton Weinmüller);

10   The nymphs of Flora (by Beyer);

11   Bacchant and priestess of Bacchus (by Beyer); together with their companion pieces on the west side, the figures flank the central avenue. They belong to the retinue of Bacchus and Flora and are the protectresses of agriculture, the fundament of the weal of state.

12   Apollo, god of the fine arts and prophecy (by Beyer);

13   Hygieia, godess of health, with a snake (by Hagenauer); a statue representing her father Aesculapius stands opposite.

14   Vestal Priestess (by Hagenauer and Posch); Like their companion pieces on the other side, these figures

Veit Kininger:
Aesculapius

Johann Baptist
Hagenauer, Jakob
Chr. Schletterer:
Queen Artemisia

symbolise the arts as well as physical and mental wellbeing, both of which promote the common weal.

15   Paris, prince of Troy, as a shepherd holding the apple of Discord in his hand (by Veit Kininger);

16   Hannibal, general of the Carthaginians (by Hagenauer); We have now crossed the parterre and have arrived at the Neptune Fountain. The series of statues continues with the figure of the great hunter Meleager. His statue is on the other side, next to the entrance to the Zoo, the former small pheasant enclosure and the game reserve, i.e. on the side of the park

dedicated to the realm of Nature. From here we follow the series of statues back to the palace.

17   Meleager, the hunter of the Chalcedonian boar (by Beyer);

18   Mercury, the flute-playing god of commerce (by Platzer);

19   Priestess with sacrificial bowl (by Weinmüller);

20   The Cumaean Sibyll, the Roman prophetess (by Beyer, Lang and Hagenauer);

21   Aesculapius, god of healing, with the caduceus (by Kininger);

22   Priestess with sacrificial baskets (by Hagenauer);

23   Priestess with sacrificial baskets (by Hagenauer);

24   Hercules in the service of Omphale (by Platzer);

25   Perseus with the snakeshead of the Gorgon Medusa (by Beyer and Wilhelm Zächerl);

26   Fabius Maximus Cunctator, Roman general (by Hagenauer);

Together with Jason and Angerona (opposite), they embody boldness and wisdom, the principles of good government.

27   Flora, Roman goddess of flowers (by Beyer);

28   The Rape of Helen by Paris (by Beyer);

29   Janus, the two-faced god of peace and Bellona, the goddess of war (by Beyer);

30   Mars, the god of war and Minerva, the goddess of peaceful arts (by Kininger);

31   Amphion, the consummate musician, moves even the stones with his lyre (by Hagenauer);

32   Mucius Scaevola, the Roman hero, who held his hand in the flames of the sacrificial altar in order to show his contempt for death (by Johann Martin Fischer);

We now cross the parterre and return to Artemisia, where our mythological tour began. Behind her, in a seemingly inaccessible part of the park, is a particularly beautiful figural group, one of Beyer's masterpieces.

33   Olympia with her son, Alexander the Great. Here, too, similarity with members of the court was detected in the features of Joseph II and his first wife, Isabella of Parma (by Beyer);

Close by there stands a charming monument to the Habsburg sense of family:

34   Bronze vase with a medallion of Queen Maria Karolina of Naples and four of her children. The queen had this simple monument erected on the site of her childhood garden. On the back is the inscription »*This rural monument is dedicated to a childlike tenderness for the immortal Maria Theresa, to the love of our dear Fatherland, to the glad memory of the joys of a carefree youth, at the place she once tended as a child, now in the circle of her children, Maria Carolina, Queen of the Two Sicilies, in her presence in the year 1802.*« (by Franz Thaller);

But now let us return to Maria Theresa's plans for the gardens and their realisation by Hohenberg.

Around 1775 the work had reached its height. Beyer's statues had been gradually erected in the park, initially not in their final order and not yet in the niches of the clipped avenues but accessible from all sides. The erection of the first completed

Johann Baptist Hagenauer: Trophies on the steps leading up to the Gloriette

The Neptune Fountain, designed by Ferdinand von Hohenberg.

The Palace Gardens

statue, that representing Artemisia, was celebrated with a gun salute and a formal dedication ceremony.

Meanwhile Hohenberg had had the grounds levelled and terraced and part of the hill removed. Two ponds were dug either side of the Gloriette as water reservoirs - the original plan was to have these linked by an underground canal upon which small boats could be paddled to and fro - and in 1775 the Gloriette was built.

This temple of fame is a tripartite Classicistic colonnaded building with Doric columns. Stone staircases inside lead up to a balustraded terrace which offers a unique panoramic view over Vienna, continuing in a south-easterly direction to the Leitha hills which once marked the border to Hungary. The interior of the Gloriette is richly decorated with sculptures and

Friedrich August Brand: The statues for the Gloriette being carved in the palace gardens. Chalk drawing, c. 1775.

The Palace Gardens

stucco work by the Italian artist Benedict Henrici and the exterior with massive trophies, together with huge vases both in niches and on the balustrade which were executed by Johann Baptist Hagenauer. Later it was said of the »*monstrous weapons, here, in a place where all around only the blessings of peace are to be seen*« that »*they do not make the best impression.*« The central part of the Gloriette bears an inscription naming Emperor Joseph II and Empress Maria Theresa as regents, as well as the date 1775.

The Gloriette was built using columns taken from the ruins of the Neugebäude, a former imperial summer residence situated to the south-east of Vienna.

The Gloriette is open to all sides to give the impression of a Mediterranean temple. This was not always greatly appreciated since in the nature of things the climatic conditions were often unsuitable. For this reason the central section was glazed a few years later so that people could sit there protected from the wind and draughts. There are plans to recreate this in the near future.

Here one should remember that in the course of two centuries many famous people have made their way to this lofty eminence and looked out over Vienna: Haydn and Mozart, Grillparzer and Beethoven, Raimund and Schubert to name only a few.

In imperial times a sparsely-wooded area extended behind the Gloriette where the young archdukes were instructed in the rudiments of hunting. The kennels for the dogs of Empress Elisabeth were also situated here.

After 1918 this area was opened to the public, but unfortunately a barracks was later constructed on this site.

Johann Christian Wilhelm Beyer: The nymph Egeria at the »Schöner Brunnen«

At the foot of the hill at Schönbrunn Hohenberg constructed a large basin which is crowned by a monumental figural group by the sculptor Franz Anton Zauner. Neptune, the Roman god of life-giving water and the sea, holds sway with his trident over the animated drama of his horse-taming companions, the Tritons. Beside him is the sea-nymph Thetis. For the delectation of gods and mortals, Hohenberg incorporated jets of water and cascades which, however, can only be activated on rare occasions due to the lack of water that Schönbrunn has always suffered from. In 1994 the Neptune Fountain underwent thorough restoration.

And yet water has played such an important role in the history of Schönbrunn! East of the Neptune Fountain, concealed in an ornamental shrubbery, is a grotto-like fountain containing the legendary spring of Schönbrunn. It was built in 1758 on the site of an earlier structure and later altered again, probably by Isidore Canevale.

The grotto housing the well preserves the stone with the monogramme of Emperor Matthias (illustrated on p. 10), who is supposed to have discovered the spring while hunting, as well as a beautiful marble sculpture commissioned from Wilhelm Beyer by Maria Theresa. The artist chose as his subject the Ancient Roman nymph Egeria, who according to myth gave counsel to the peace-loving Numa Pompilius, the second of Rome's legendary kings. There was a grotto dedicated to her on the Via Appia, the site of which is today still called the »*bosco sacro*« or sacred wood.

From an urn Egeria dispenses the much-praised water, the use of which was strictly regulated, even for the imperial family. It provided the drinking water of Emperor Franz Joseph and Empress Elisabeth, not only at Schönbrunn but also at the Hofburg and even when they were travelling!
The water of Schönbrunn, »the best in Austria«, was even taken as far as Jerusalem in a soldered metal box on one of the Emperor's journeys, and it was brought daily to the Hofburg by a team of mules.
Near the well we find three further statues by Beyer. Opposite stands
35 Cybele, the »Great Mother« of all life; her mural crown identifies her as the protectress of a city. She is also a figure of grief and seeks solitude, accompanied only by two lions (by Beyer).

Under the trees on the diagonal avenue leading away from the Naiad Fountain two seated figures are concealed:
36 Cincinnatus, Roman general; the farmer Cincinnatus was summoned from his plough to be a general and dictator. He is fastening his sandals in order to follow the call of his fatherland (by Beyer);
37 Euridice, wife of Orpheus; she puts her hand over the snake bite which will bring about her death (by Beyer).
We now approach the Obelisk, the towering height of which has been visible for some time. But before we examine it, let us look at the last work in the series of statues:
38 Roman matron; in this figure of a venerable Roman wife, Hagenauer has created a symbol of civic virtue and religious

piety. An especially beautiful feature and one which evinces the consummate skill of the artist is the hair braided into a six-stranded plait (by Hagenauer).

The Obelisk, which Hohenberg created in 1772 as an effective addition to the other architectural structures on the park, is typical of the age of Classicism, with its romantic and sentimental recreation of »noble« antiquity.

A semicircular structure encloses a pool. Above the grotto recline river gods who allegedly symbolise the confluence of the Enns and the Danube. At the centre, from a socle with four turtles rises the Obelisk, decorated with mock hiero-

glyphics which purportedly relate the history of the House of Habsburg.

On the large avenue leading back to the Neptune Fountain, again intended as a picturesque view to be seen from the Naiad fountain, stand the Roman Ruins.

This extraordinary structure is proof of Hohenberg's inventive imagination and consummate mastery of execution. Paintings with fantastic ruins as a motif had already been popular in the Baroque, but it was the Romantic Age which actually built them. Many examples of this type of ruin can be found in the environs of Vienna. The ruins at Schönbrunn occupy a curious position between Baroque stage set and Romantic *veduta* and are intended to evoke the impression of a genuine ruin from classical antiquity.

In front of the ruins, which open out like a stage, lies an overgrown pool, creating a compelling distance between

spectator and structure. In the water is a figural group by Beyer representing the confluence of the Vltava and Elbe rivers. Few works of architecture have made such a deep impression on contemporaries and posterity as this sentimental monument to decay, set in the middle of a Baroque landscape representing Nature as ordered by the human mind.

The Palace Gardens

The Palace Gardens